LOTUS 1-2-3
version 2.3 & 2.4
Training Guide

Graham Taylor

PITMAN
PUBLISHING

PITMAN PUBLISHING
128 Long Acre, London, WC2E 9AN

A Division of Longman Group UK Limited

© Graham Taylor 1993

First published in Great Britain 1993

British Library Cataloguing-in-Publication Data
A catalogue record for this book is available from the British Library.

ISBN 0-273-03741-2

Printed and bound in Great Britain.

Acknowledgement

Bill Smith for the use of his exercise in Task 42 and Yvonne Siouty for her considerable assistance.

Contents

Introduction

Lotus 1-2-3

Lotus 1-2-3 is an integrated business applications package combining a spreadsheet with graphics and data management. The best selling micro-computer package to date, Lotus 1-2-3, is comprehensive, yet easy to use.

What is a spreadsheet package?

A spreadsheet lets you analyse and work with numbers and formulae which are organised in columns and rows. A spreadsheet is the electronic equivalent of an accountant's ledger - a large piece of paper divided by vertical columns and horizontal rows into a grid of cells. The user may enter *numbers*, *formulae* or *text* directly into each of these cells.

Each cell is referred to by its co-ordinates, like a map-reference or point on a graph e.g. cell C12 is in column C and row 12. *Formulae* may be entered to link cells e.g. B1*C1 multiplies the contents of cells B1 and C1 - and formulae provide the wherewithal to keep totals in a spreadsheet 'up-to-date' automatically.

Uses

Spreadsheets are flexible modelling tools which can be adapted for many jobs involving repetitive numerical calculations, for example:

- Financial plans and budgets can be represented as a table, with columns for time periods (months) and rows for different elements of the plan (costs and revenues).
- Tax, investment and loan calculations.
- Statistics - average, standard deviation, time series and regression analysis (in-built functions are included).
- Consolidation - merging branch or departmental accounts to form group (consolidated) accounts. This involves merging two or more worksheets together.
- Currency conversion - useful for an organisation with overseas interests such as a multi-national company.
- Data can be converted into effective display graphs of various types.

What..if analysis

Any figure can be changed at any time and, providing the correct formula is in place, the new results will be automatically shown. This is called "what if" analysis. For example, *what if* sales go up by 10%? Increase the total sales figure and other linked entries (e.g. profit totals) will adjust automatically. It is this facility to quickly recalculate figures which makes spreadsheets such powerful, useful and popular programs.

New features in Lotus 1-2-3 version 2.3 and 2.4

- New graph types and better control over graph appearance - a 3-D effect.
- New printing features, background printer and the facility to save printer instructions in an encoded file.
- New worksheet features - the facility to save display colours (using *Wysiwyg*) and better use of expanded memory.
- Improved search and replace facility in a range.
- Better criteria formula specification in database searches.
- Other new features include:

  mouse support; dialog boxes; the facility to specify a range before you select a command; the facility to edit the current file directory; new macro commands; use of the delete key DEL to delete contents of current cell; a context-sensitive help system; and, improved prompts.
- New add-in features:

  Wysiwyg for enhanced spreadsheet publishing
  Viewer to view the contents of disk files
  Auditor to identify and check worksheet formulae

Version 2.4 includes all the new features of 2.3 and adds the following:

- SmartIcons add-in
- Backsolver add-in
- SmartPics
- Landscape print facility for all printers
- PostScript file print facility

WYSIWYG

Lotus 1-2-3 versions 2.3 and 2.4 also include a program called *Wysiwyg* which enables you to format, print and edit your work in a variety of ways. *Wysiwyg* stands for '**W**hat **y**ou **s**ee **i**s **w**hat **y**ou **g**et'! It can make a big difference to how your work looks. Lotus refers to it as its spreadsheet publishing *add-in*. There are also two on-line tutorials supplied with the package. These are *1-2-3 Go!* and *Wysiwyg-Go!* which aim to show you the basic skills and concepts of the programs. Once you have worked through them it is recommended that you delete these tutorial files to regain 2Mb of disk space.

Versions 2.3 and 2.4 require:

- an IBM *or* IBM-compatible personal computer
- a hard disk and diskette drive
- about 2Mb of disk space for 1-2-3; about 5Mb if you include the add-in programs
- a monochrome *or* (preferably) colour monitor
- a keyboard
- 384K of main memory (*or* 512K with the add-in programs)
- version 2.1 or above of the Disk Operating System (DOS)
- a mouse (optional)

Lotus versions 2.01, 2.2, 2.3 and 2.4

Version 2.3 is compatible with earlier versions of the package so most of the exercises in this *Guide* will apply as well to versions 2.01 or 2.2 with only very minor differences. However, the *Wysiwyg* tasks relate to versions 2.3 and 2.4 only.

Conventions The following conventions are used throughout this *Guide*:

Function keys are given their 1-2-3 name and shown in boxes e.g. HELP F1

Key names joined by the - sign mean that you must press and hold down the first key while pressing the second key e.g. CTRL-LEFT ARROW (i.e. CONTROL key with LEFT ARROW key)

Where function key names follow sequentially but are separated by a space, press the first key and then press the second e.g. END HOME

Information that you are to type in appears in bold typeface
e.g. **INTEREST RATE CALCULATION**

The ENTER key is used throughout the guide; the RETURN key does the same job. Press the ENTER or RETURN key on your keyboard whenever you see the symbol ENTER

Getting started

It is assumed that Lotus 1-2-3 and the add-in feature Wysiwyg have been installed on the hard disk of your computer in a directory called 123R24 (123R23 for version 2.3)

From the **DOS C:>** prompt:

1   TYPE **CD\123R24** and PRESS ENTER to enter the 1-2-3 directory.
2   TYPE **123** and PRESS ENTER to go directly into the Lotus 1-2-3 worksheet.

A blank spreadsheet will be displayed on your screen. You are now ready to begin working your way through the *Guide*.

Short cut

A batch file stores and executes a series of commands when invoked. It may be useful to set up a **batch file** called **123.BAT** so that Lotus 1-2-3 can be loaded automatically from the operating system prompt.
To do this you can create the following batch file using any text editor:

C:
CD \123R24   change directory to 123R24
123   123 exe file (or LOTUS - *see* below)
**CD **   returns to root directory when you quit the program

Refer to your Operating System user guide for more information.

Note: Lotus 1-2-3 has two executable files to start-up the program:

123.EXE   - loads the worksheet
LOTUS.EXE   - loads the Access menu with options of 123, PrintGraph, Translate and Install

To use these facilities TYPE **LOTUS** and PRESS ENTER at the DOS prompt in the Lotus 123 directory. If you frequently need to translate files between Lotus 1-2-3 and other programs, print graphs or change equipment selections (e.g. printer) then you may prefer to use the LOTUS start-up in your batch file.

Section A: First things first ▪▪▪▪▪▪▪▪▪▪

Task 1   **Looking and moving around the spreadsheet screen**

Objectives   To become familiar with the worksheet screen.
To move around the worksheet.

Instructions   If you have not already done so, follow the instructions in *Getting started* to enter Lotus 1-2-3. A blank spreadsheet will appear on your screen.

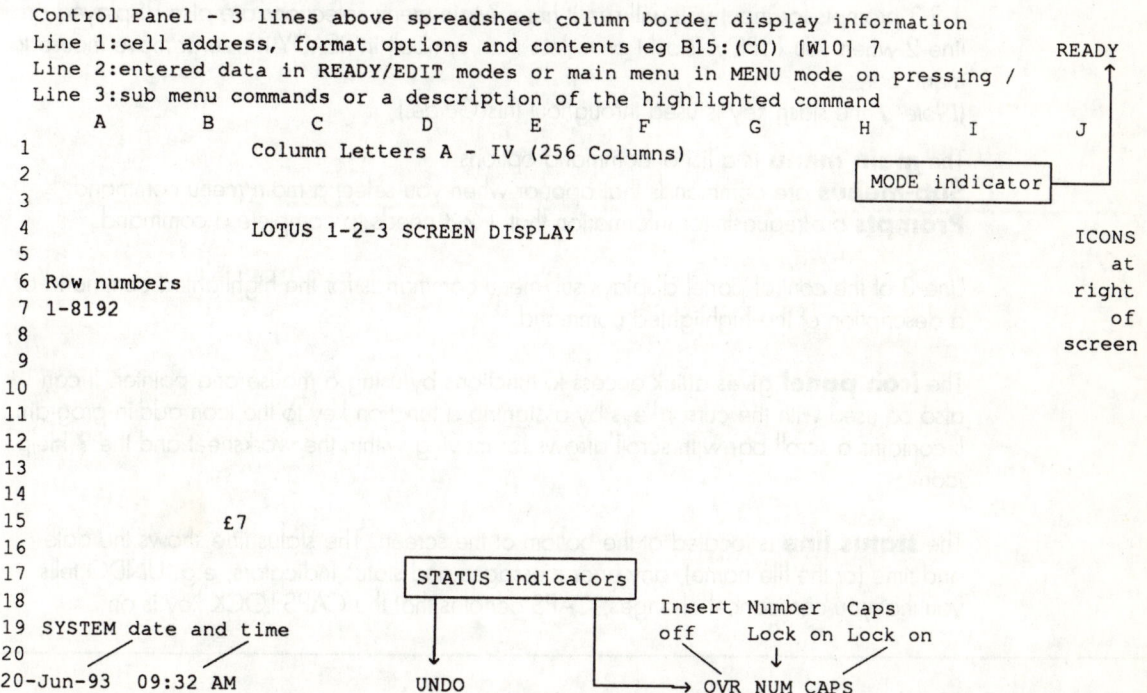

```
Control Panel - 3 lines above spreadsheet column border display information
Line 1:cell address, format options and contents eg B15:(C0) [W10] 7        READY
Line 2:entered data in READY/EDIT modes or main menu in MENU mode on pressing /
Line 3:sub menu commands or a description of the highlighted command
     A       B        C        D        E        F        G        H        I        J
 1                   Column Letters A - IV (256 Columns)
 2                                                          ┌────────────────────┐
 3                                                          │  MODE indicator    │
 4                   LOTUS 1-2-3 SCREEN DISPLAY             └────────────────────┘
 5                                                                              ICONS
 6  Row numbers                                                                   at
 7  1-8192                                                                      right
 8                                                                                of
 9                                                                            screen
10
11
12
13
14
15              £7
16
17                          ┌─────────────────────┐
18                          │ STATUS indicators   │
19  SYSTEM date and time    └─────────────────────┘   Insert  Number  Caps
20                                                      off    Lock on Lock on
20-Jun-93  09:32 AM              UNDO                           ↓      ↓
                                                       OVR NUM CAPS
```

The **worksheet** - a grid of columns and rows - takes up most of the Lotus display screen. This is where you enter and work with data.

The entire worksheet is too large to fit on your screen. There are 256 columns (lettered A..Z, AA..AZ, BA..BZ up to IV) and 8192 rows (numbered 1..8192). However, you will soon see how easy it is to move to any part of the spreadsheet that you need. The intersection of every column and row is called a **cell**. Each cell is referenced by a column letter(s) followed by a row number. This is known as the **cell address** e.g. A1, B7, DR99. The rectangular bar which highlights the position of the current cell is called the **cell pointer**.

The **control panel** is used for communication and interactive purposes. It consists of three lines at the top of the screen showing information about the currently active cell and about commands i.e. actions you tell 1-2-3 to perform from a menu.

1

Line 1 of the control panel gives the cell address, contents, format, protection status, mode indicator and column width.

The **cell format** refers to the way in which values are shown e.g. number of decimal places.

The **protection status**, when on, will show **U** if the cell is unprotected and **PR** if the cell is protected i.e. the contents cannot be overwritten.

The **column width** is the number of characters that 1-2-3 will display in the cell if you have changed it from the initial 9 characters.

The **mode indicator** (READY, MENU, VALUE, WAIT etc) is at the top right of the screen. It changes to tell you what state (mode) 1-2-3 is in. For example, if you type a number, 1-2-3's mode indicator becomes VALUE.

Line 2 of the control panel is where data entry is displayed as you type in or edit data. If 1-2-3 prompts for input you will see it here. Main menu selections are also displayed on line 2 when you TYPE **/** (slash) or **<** (less than symbol) in READY mode or move mouse to menu bar.
(*Note:* **/** the slash key is used throughout this *Guide*.)

The **main menu** is a list of command options.

Sub-menus are commands that appear when you select a main menu command.

Prompts are requests for information that 1-2-3 needs to complete a command.

Line 3 of the control panel displays sub-menu commands for the highlighted command or a description of the highlighted command.

The **icon panel** gives quick access to functions by using a mouse and pointer. It can also be used with the cursor keys by assigning a function key to the Icon add-in program. It contains a scroll bar with scroll arrows for moving within the worksheet and the **?** Help icon

The **status line** is located at the bottom of the screen. The status line shows the date and time (or the file name), any error messages and status indicators, e.g. UNDO tells you that you can cancel changes; CAPS denotes that the CAPS LOCK key is on.

Activty 1.1 Moving around the worksheet

The cell pointer can be moved from cell to cell with the pointer-movement (arrow) keys which are on the right hand side of your keyboard.

1   To use these keys ensure that **NumLock** is **off**. Many keyboards have a light above the key showing whether it is on or off. PRESS it if it is on.

2   PRESS each of the arrow keys - LEFT ARROW , RIGHT ARROW , UP ARROW , and DOWN ARROW in turn for practice. These pointer-movement keys move the cell pointer up or down, right or left.

3   PRESS F5 (the Goto function key), TYPE **AA99** and PRESS ENTER . The cell pointer is now in cell AA99.

You can jump directly to any cell in the spreadsheet in this way.

4   PRESS the HOME key. This returns you to the top left (cell A1).

5   PRESS END RIGHT ARROW (End then right arrow). This moves you to IV1 - the top right of your spreadsheet.

6   PRESS END DOWN ARROW (End then down arrow) to take you to the bottom right corner i.e. cell IV8192.

Note: when working with a spreadsheet which contains data the END RIGHT ARROW and END LEFT ARROW keys will take you to the borders of your spreadsheet work - known as the **active area**. This is the point at which cell entries finish and blank cells appear. Conversely if you are in a blank area, these keys will stop at the first non-blank cell.

7   PRESS HOME to return to A1.

PgUp moves up 20 rows.
PgDn moves down 20 rows.
TAB moves right 8 columns.
SHIFT-TAB moves left 8 columns.

Alternatively, you can use CTRL-RIGHT ARROW and CTRL-LEFT ARROW instead of TAB and SHIFT-TAB .

Moving the cell pointer off the end of the displayed worksheet either vertically or horizontally is known as scrolling. As you scroll, new columns or row labels appear and others go away. Do not panic, you can always get back to them; they are not lost.

Mouse users should note that there are 10 icons in palette 4 to help you move about the screen. To see what each does PRESS and HOLD DOWN the right mouse button on the selected icon.

An icon reference table appears in Task 37.

Task 2   **Mouse, menus and dialog boxes**

Objective   To use the mouse and the keyboard to select menus and access dialog boxes.

Instructions   Most tasks in 1-2-3 require you to select commands from menus. Menus appear in the control panel when you TYPE $\boxed{/}$ (the slash key).
They have a multi-level structure. While only one level at a time is shown, more than one selection may often be necessary. Using the keyboard there are 2 methods of choosing a command.

- **Point**
  With the menu titles on display in the control panel, you can use the cursor keys $\boxed{\text{RIGHT ARROW}}$, $\boxed{\text{LEFT ARROW}}$, $\boxed{\text{HOME}}$ and $\boxed{\text{END}}$ to move and highlight the command that you want. Press $\boxed{\text{ENTER}}$ to select the command highlighted. This method is recommended for beginners. It takes a little longer but you can see information about your chosen command on the line below. This will either be a sub-menu or a description of the command.

- **Type**
  Type the first character of the command. If you make a mistake or change your mind. Press the $\boxed{\text{ESC}}$ (Escape) key to return to the previous menu. Selection will cause changes in the control panel. A sub-menu will appear on line 2 and new comments on line 3. You can continue to make selections or use $\boxed{\text{ESC}}$ to go back one step at a time. $\boxed{\text{CTRL-BREAK}}$ will cancel all of the **command sequence** at once. More than one menu selection represents a command sequence. Try the following simple Activity.

Activity 2.1 Changing the current directory

Files you create during Lotus 1-2-3 sessions will be saved to the current directory (C:\123R24) unless you specify another directory to use.

1. Request the main menu: PRESS $\boxed{/}$ (slash) key.

2. HIGHLIGHT **F**(ile) and then **D**(irectory). To do this use the $\boxed{\text{ARROW}}$ **keys** and PRESS $\boxed{\text{ENTER}}$.

3. Lotus prompts: **Enter current directory: C:\123R24**.

4. PRESS $\boxed{\text{ESC}}$ 3 times if you are happy with the present directory or if you have made a mistake.

5. Insert a floppy disk into drive A, TYPE **A:** and PRESS $\boxed{\text{ENTER}}$ *or* the drive letter and directory name that you want.

Files will now be saved to and retrieved from diskette drive A in the current work session. *See* Activity 5.5 if you wish to make the directory change permanent.

Dialog boxes

Some 1-2-3 commands such as **/W**(orksheet) **G**(lobal) require the selection of additional commands to specify a number of settings. In such cases 1-2-3 displays a dialog box.

A **Dialog** (or settings) **box** is a special screen that helps you to keep track of the changes you make to certain worksheet settings. Headings correspond to commands in the control panel but more information is given in the box. It is a useful alternative to using the menus when several settings have to be changed at once.

Popup dialog boxes appear over a dialog box when a selection leads to a further series of choices.

Activty 2.2 Using a dialog box

One example of a dialog box is the Global Settings dialog box. This helps the user make changes to the appearance of all (global) spreadsheet entries. By way of a demonstration you will enter some data, widen all the columns to 12 characters (default 9), hide (blank out) all zeros and display all figures significant to 2 decimal places.

1   SELECT **/W**(orksheet)**G**(lobal)

The Global Settings dialog box will appear. Asterisks denote that an **option button** is selected; an X denotes that a check box is selected.

2   PRESS F2 (function key F2, the Edit key).

3   MOVE to the setting you want to change with the arrow keys or TYPE the highlighted letter.

4   PRESS **C** for Column width.

5   TYPE **12** ENTER to change all column widths to 12 characters.

6   SELECT **Z**(ero display)**B**(lank).

7   SELECT **F**(ormat). A popup dialog box appears.

8   SELECT **Fixed**. Accept **2** decimal places and PRESS ENTER.

9   SELECT **OK** - the **command button** - which confirms that you want to use the new settings or SELECT **Cancel** to cancel the changes.

10 PRESS ESC three times to return to your worksheet.

Note: all columns are now 12 characters wide and zero will not be displayed.

11 TYPE in a long label (your name if it is over 12 characters long) into cell A1 and TYPE **0** in any cell and PRESS ENTER.

Note: the zero is blanked (hidden) but is shown in the control panel.

12 TYPE **23** in cell B1 and PRESS ENTER.

Note: the display 23.00 - significant to 2 decimal places.

Now reset the global default settings to 9 characters column-width, zeros displayed and integer numbers.

13 SELECT **/ W**(orksheet) **G**(lobal).

14 PRESS F2 .

15 SELECT **C**.

16 TYPE **9** ENTER.

17 SELECT **Zero display**.

18 SELECT **Zeros**.

19 SELECT **Format General**.

20 SELECT **OK** and ESC ESC ESC to the worksheet.

21 SELECT **/ W**(orksheet) **G**(lobal) **Default Update** if you want to save the settings changes on file.

Using a mouse

In 1-2-3 version 2.3 and 2.4 you can use a mouse for many standard tasks, for example you can:

- move the cell pointer
- select menu commands
- specify ranges of cells
- select and mark items in dialog boxes
- select Help topics

When *Wysiwyg* is attached, the mouse has extra capabilities, including graphics editing and changing the column width or row height.

To use a mouse, you must be familiar with the following actions and terms:

CLICK: PRESS the mouse button and release it. Do *not* hold the mouse button down.
DOUBLE CLICK: PRESS the mouse button *twice* in quick succession.
SELECT: CLICK the left mouse button. CLICK the right mouse button to cancel (same effect as pressing ESC).
DRAG: PRESS and HOLD DOWN the mouse button, MOVE the mouse and then RELEASE the mouse button.

Throughout this *Guide* assume that the left button is used unless otherwise stated. Some Tasks make specific use of the mouse and in these cases mouse instructions are given. With most Tasks, however, it is a matter of personal choice as to whether you use the keyboard or mouse or a combination of both.

Mouse Methods are as follows:

To start the main menu:
Simply MOVE the mouse pointer to the control panel.

To start the *Wysiwyg* menu (this assumes *Wysiwyg* is attached *see* Task 33:
MOVE the mouse pointer to the control panel. CLICK the **right** button. CLICK right again to switch back to main menu.

To move the menu pointer:
DRAG the mouse pointer along the menu selections. RELEASE the button while pointing at the highlighted command that you want. If you do not want to select MOVE the pointer away from the control panel and then release the button.

To select a menu option:
CLICK on command to select. For example, to display the full-screen list of names in *files* mode,
CLICK **LIST** in the first line of the control panel.
CLICK right button to cancel the menu command.

To accept a response to a prompt:
CLICK the control panel.

To enter a response to a prompt:
TYPE the **response** and CLICK the **control panel** e.g. PRESS F5 (Goto), TYPE **A99** and CLICK on the cell reference.

To specify a range of cells:
MOVE the mouse pointer to the upper left cell of range.
DRAG the mouse to highlight the required range.

To select dialog box options:
CLICK the **option(s)**.

To select an item from a list box in a dialog box:
CLICK a **scroll arrow** in the icon panel to scroll through the list. CLICK on **item** name.

To cancel a command:
CLICK the **right** mouse button as often as necessary.

To back up one menu level:
CLICK the **right** mouse button *or* CLICK **cancel** in a **dialog box**.

From now on keystroke instructions will tell you to select a command as follows:

TYPE **/**(the slash key) **F**(ile) **L**(ist) to list files.

It is your choice whether to **point** and PRESS ENTER *or* CLICK the mouse button *or* TYPE the first character of the command. Remember the point method is best for beginners.

Key words	Spreadsheet	Mode indicator
	Cell	Main menu
	Cell address	Sub menu
	Cell pointer	Prompt
	Current cell	Icon panel
	Control panel	Status line
	Cell format	Active area
	Protection status	Dialog box
	Column width	Mouse

Task 3   **Help**

Objective   To access and use the Help system.

Instructions   1-2-3 has a context sensitive Help system that explains your current action. Help includes an index, a series of procedures (how do I ...?) and a glossary of 1-2-3 terms.

Activity 3.1 Getting Help in 1-2-3

1   PRESS the HELP key $\boxed{\text{F1}}$ or CLICK the **?** (Help icon).

2   HIGHLIGHT a topic e.g. **Dialog Boxes** and PRESS $\boxed{\text{ENTER}}$.

3   EXPERIMENT as you wish.

4   PRESS $\boxed{\text{ESC}}$ or CLICK **right** to leave Help.

5   PRESS $\boxed{\text{CTRL-F1}}$ (bookmark). This displays the last Help screen you were looking at. It is helpful to use this bookmark feature when you have forgotten what you have just read. Again, PRESS $\boxed{\text{ESC}}$ to return to the worksheet.

As you begin to master the package you will find the Help facility increasingly useful. It is a 'context sensitive' HELP, i.e. it tries to help you where you get stuck! For example,

6   SELECT **Save** from the **File menu** (**/F**(ile)**S**(ave)).

7   PRESS $\boxed{\text{F1}}$. Help appears with information about entering a file name when saving your work.

8   PRESS $\boxed{\text{ESC}}$ (or $\boxed{\text{ESC}}$ $\boxed{\text{Ctrl-BREAK}}$) 6 *times* to return to the worksheet.

9   TYPE **/** (the slash key) **Q**(uit) **Y**(es) to leave 1-2-3. Do this whenever you wish to finish a session.

9

Section B: Spreadsheet essentials ■■■■■■

Task 4

Entering data

Objective To enter text (*labels*), numbers (*values*) and a formula by completing a simple activity.

Instructions Start up 1-2-3 or if you have continued from the previous Task PRESS **/ W**(orksheet) **E**(rase) **Y**(es) to delete data and restore default settings.

You will now be faced with an empty spreadsheet, with the cell in the top left hand corner highlighted by the cell pointer. Any entry you make will be typed on the second line of the screen and will be put into the current cell when you press ENTER . If you make a mistake, press the DEL (Delete) key to delete the contents of a cell. *See* Task 6 for more help on correcting mistakes.

Activity 4.1 Entering labels, values and formulae

1   In cell **A1** TYPE **DATA ENTRY DEMONSTRATION** and PRESS ENTER.

Note how the text extends beyond the 9 character width of the cell. This is known as a long label.

2   PRESS DOWN ARROW twice, TYPE **SALES** in cell **A3** and PRESS DOWN ARROW .

3   TYPE **COST** and PRESS DOWN ARROW .

4   TYPE **PROFIT** and PRESS RIGHT ARROW . The cell pointer should now be in cell B5.

5   TYPE **+B3-B4** and PRESS UP ARROW .

You have just entered a formula! 1-2-3 however just shows you its result, and as there are no values in B3 and B4, in this case it is zero.

6   TYPE a number into B4, PRESS UP ARROW , then TYPE another number into B3, and PRESS ENTER .

You now have a spreadsheet with **labels** (in A1, A3, A4 and A5), **values** (in B3 and B4) and a **formula** to be evaluated (in B5). On a micro scale this is what spreadsheets are all about.

7   Try altering the figures in the SALES and COST cells; use the arrow keys to position the cell pointer, TYPE a value and PRESS ENTER or ARROW to insert it. Note how PROFIT is immediately recalculated.

You can enter **one** of three items in a cell: a **value**, a **formula** or a **label**.

A value

- is data which can be used in calculations
- it must start with a numeral 0 to 9, a + (plus) or a - (minus sign) or a decimal point (.) or £, $ currency symbols
- may take the form of a number in Scientific notation (e.g. 1.234E+06)
- may end with a percent sign (%)
- is right aligned and the alignment of a value cannot be changed
- spaces, commas or other punctuation (except for the decimal point) should not be entered

For practice, TYPE in adjacent cells **7**, **£9**, **-8**, **.9**, **1.234e+06**, **23%**.

A formula

- mathematical formulae or functions that calculate values
- must indicate a mathematical operation e.g. (10+5)*A1
- must start with a numeral or with **+ - (@**.
- **mathematical operators are** **+** plus, **-** minus, ***** multiply, **/** divide, **^** to the power of

For practice,   **Result**

in cell E1 TYPE **123+1**, PRESS DOWN ARROW	124
in E2 TYPE **+E1*10**, PRESS DOWN ARROW	1240
in E3 TYPE **+E1+E2**, PRESS DOWN ARROW	1364
in E4 TYPE **(E2-E1)*E3**, PRESS ENTER	1522224

Activity 4.2 Rather than typing formulae, you can also enter formulae by pointing to the relevant cells using cursor keys or mouse click. Having entered the formulae above:

1 MOVE to **E5** and TYPE **+**.

2 MOVE to **E4**. The mode indicator now displays POINT. The cell address and contents appear in the control panel. TYPE **+**.

3 MOVE to **E3**. TYPE **+**.

4 TYPE **100** and PRESS ENTER.

The formulae are shown in the control panel and the result appears in the cell. The result, 1523688 will appear in cell **E5**.

1-2-3 has many built-in functions for statistical, financial and other work. They begin with the @ sign, e.g. **@SUM(B4..F4)** will add the contents of cells B4 through to F4. You will use the more popular functions later on in the *Guide*.

A label

- is text in alphanumeric characters used to give titles or headings to numeric data
- can contain any string of characters or numbers
- must begin with a letter of the alphabet or a symbol except those which indicate a number or a formula or are otherwise used by 1-2-3 (e.g. /+ # @)
- may be up to 240 characters long
- may display accross several worksheet columns. If the next column is occupied, 1-2-3 displays as many characters as possible and stores the rest. 1-2-3 automatically places the defualt label prefix ' (apostrophe) at the beginning of each label. This is the label-prefix. It appears in the control panel but not in the worksheet.
- to enter a label which begins with a number first PRESS a **label-prefix** character. This will also position the label in the cell as follows:

' (apostrophe)	left-justify text (default)
" (double quote)	right-justify
^ (caret)	centre

Activity 4.3 Aligning labels

TYPE **'SALES**, **"COSTS**, **^PROFITS** in A7, A8 and A9 respectively. Remember to PRESS the ENTER and/or DOWN ARROW key after each entry. Note how they are positioned in the cells.

Key words
label
value
formula
built-in functions @
label prefix ' " ^

Task 5 — Working with files

Objectives To open, close, name, save, retrieve and erase files from disk.

Instructions For this Task you should have the simple spreadsheet created in Task 4 on screen.

Activity 5.1 Saving, naming and closing a file

1 TYPE the **/** (slash) key, then look at the menu at the top of the screen.

2 PRESS RIGHT ARROW until **File** is highlighted and PRESS ENTER.

3 PRESS **S** or use the mouse to select **Save**.

1-2-3 prompts: **ENTER name of file to save: A:*.wk1**.
Note: **C:\123R24*.WK1** appears if you have not changed the default drive.

The **A:** denotes that the A drive will be used to save your file. **** denotes DOS directory e.g. **C:\123*wk1** is in the C drive, 123 subdirectory. ***** is a wildcard. The **.WK1** is the extension which 1-2-3 will append indicating that it is a worksheet file.

4 TYPE in the filename e.g. **DEMO1** (remember to keep file names short) and PRESS ENTER. Your file is now saved on disk.

Note: filenames can be up to eight characters long with no spaces.

5 SELECT **/ W**(orksheet) **E**(rase) **Y**(es) to clear the screen for further work.

Activity 5.2 Retrieving an existing file

Your file is now on disk so you can bring it back into memory at any time.

1 SELECT **/ F**(ile) **R**(etrieve) and HIGHLIGHT the filename **DEMO1**, then PRESS ENTER. DEMO1 will be called from disk on to the screen.

When you have stored a number of files it is better to PRESS F3 after **/ File Retrieve**. This will show a full screen menu of filenames in alphabetical order. The third line of the screen shows:

- the name of the highlighted file
- date and time created
- the size of the file in kilobytes

You can either TYPE the filename that you require *or* HIGHLIGHT it by using the pointer keys before PRESSING ENTER.

Activity 5.3 Saving an existing file

1 SELECT **/ F**(ile) **R**(etrieve) **DEMO1** ENTER if you do not have the DEMO1 spreadsheet on screen.

2 In any cell TYPE: **Here is an update of the file which I am now going to save**.

3 SELECT **Q**(uit) **Y**(es).

1-2-3 prompts: **WORKSHEET CHANGES NOT SAVED! End 1-2-3 anyway?**

You have forgotten to save this vital update, so:

4 SELECT **No**.

5 SELECT **/ F**(ile) **S**(ave).

1-2-3 offers the current filename DEMO1.

6 PRESS ENTER to accept this filename.

1-2-3 prompts: **Cancel Replace Backup**

7 SELECT **B**(ackup) by pressing **B** on the keyboard or by clicking **Backup** using the mouse.

Note: Backup will keep the old version of DEMO1 on disk but rename the file DEMO1.BAK (for BAcKup) and save the new version of the file as DEMO1.WK1. Use **Backup** when you are not sure! In business applications it is always prudent to backup files. You then have something to fall back on if things go wrong.

Cancel will cancel the command and leave the original DEMO1 file on disk. Use Cancel when you wish to return to the current worksheet without saving.

Replace will overwrite the old version of DEMO1 with this new updated file. Use Replace when you do not want to keep the old file.

Activity 5.4 Erasing a file

To erase one of the files from disk, ensure that DEMO1 is in use, then:

1 SELECT **/ F**(ile) **E**(rase). Note that you can erase a worksheet, print a graph or any other file.

2 SELECT **O**(ther).

3   HIGHLIGHT **DEMO1.BAK**.

4   SELECT **Y**(es) to erase the file from disk.

Activity 5.5 Retrieving a file when you start 1-2-3

This feature is useful if you are sure of the file you need and you wish to load it straight-away. First, quit 1-2-3.

1   SELECT **/ Q**(uit) **Y**(es) to leave 1-2-3.

2   At the C:\> prompt TYPE **123 -wdemo1**. *Note*: space between **3** and **-**.

123 -wfilename will immediately retrieve the worksheet file DEMO1. The command assumes that DEMO1 is in the default directory - the directory which 1-2-3 looks at first. If you wish to change the directory:

3   SELECT **/ W**(orksheet) **G**(lobal) **D**(efault) **D**(irectory).

4   TYPE **A:** (or the directory you require) and SELECT **U**(pdate).

1-2-3 will refer to the diskette drive A: for files until you change the default setting again.

Activity 5.6 Creating a new file

1   SELECT **/ W**(orksheet) **E**(rase) **Y**(es) to clear the screen.

The previous data is cleared from 1-2-3's memory and all worksheet settings are restored to default. You are now ready to create a new worksheet.

Key words Save
Retrieve
Erase
Cancel
Replace
Backup

Task 6   Editing and correcting mistakes

Objectives   To make simple changes using the edit function key and the search and replace facility.

Instructions   If a cell entry is incorrect or needs updating it is usually convenient just to retype it and overwrite the original. In version 2.3 and 2.4 you can also delete the whole contents of the current cell by pressing DEL. However, the edit function key - F2 - provides a quick way of changing entries.

CLOSE the current file with **/ W**(orksheet) **E**(rase).

Activity 6.1 The edit function key - F2

1   In cell A1 TYPE **This is a big mustake** and PRESS ENTER.

2   PRESS F2.

3   Use ARROW key to MOVE the cursor to **u**.

4   PRESS INS to turn *insert* mode off. The OVR - *overtype* status indicator will be displayed in the status line at the bottom of the screen.

5   TYPE **i** and PRESS ENTER.

When you PRESS F2 the cell entry contents will appear on line 2 of the control panel. The ARROW (cursor) keys can be used to move around the entry. The DEL key deletes the character at the cursor, while the BACKSPACE key deletes the character at the left of the cursor. The INS key switches between inserting text, by moving existing text to the right, and replacing existing text. PRESS ENTER when complete and the edit will appear in the actual cell.

6   Practise typing long labels into cells and editing them.

Activity 6.2 Using UNDO

The UNDO feature is available in versions 2.3 and 2.4 of 1-2-3 and is *off* initially to save memory. To enable the UNDO feature:

1   SELECT **/ W**(orksheet) **G**(lobal) **D**(efault) **S**(tatus). The screen displays current default settings.

2   PRESS any key to continue.

3   PRESS F2 to edit the settings.

4   PRESS **N** for undo - the *UNDO* feature is turned *on* and an **x** is placed to mark it in the check box.

5   SELECT **U** to Update the setting.

6   SELECT **Q**(uit) to return to the worksheet.

Note: there is an alternative command sequence: **/ W**(orksheet) **G**(lobal) **D**(efault) **O**(ther) **U**(ndo) **E**(nable) **U**(pdate) **Q**(uit) which will also turn UNDO *on*. Now that UNDO is enabled you can toggle between your present spreadsheet data and the last change i.e. you have 'stored' the last thing that you did.

7 PRESS ALT-F4 (the UNDO feature.)

8 PRESS ALT-F4 again.

UNDO will cancel the most recent change made in your worksheet. Press it again to restore your last change. This is useful for retracting your last mistake.

Activity 6.3 Search and replace

1 TYPE **Gary Linaker** in cells C1, C2 and C3.

2 SELECT **/ R**(ange) **S**(earch).

3 TYPE **C1..C3** *or* HIGHLIGHT **C1..C3** and PRESS ENTER.

1-2-3 prompts: **Enter string to search for:**

4 TYPE **ak**.

5 SELECT **L**(abels) **R**(eplace).

1-2-3 prompts: **Enter replacement string:**

6 TYPE **ek**.

7 SELECT **A**(ll).

Note: all three cells are changed to the correct spelling. What would have happened if you had selected **a** and **e** as the search and replacement strings? Go back to the original spelling and try it out. *See also* Activity 9.2.

Key words **F2**   **ALT-F4**
         Edit   **Search**
         DEL   **Replace**
         UNDO

17

Copying and moving

Objectives   To copy cells using the copy command.
To move cell contents to a different cell.

Instructions   **Copying using the keyboard**

The **Copy** command creates copies of existing cell entries. When formulae are copied or moved the cell addresses contained in the formula are automatically adjusted to the new cell location. A **range** of cell(s) is a single cell or a block of cells. For more information on ranges see Task 9.

To perform the action of copying the contents of one or more cells, first position the cell pointer in the first cell to be copied and select the **Copy** command from the control panel. 1-2-3 will prompt: **Copy what?** and indicates the cell in which the cell pointer is currently positioned. Highlight the range of cells to copy using ARROW keys and press ENTER. 1-2-3 then prompts: **To where?** *Either* type in the cell range (e.g. C7..F12) or highlight it and press ENTER.

Highlighting a cell range to copy into

Move the cell pointer to the beginning of the target range and type **.** (full stop) to anchor the cell pointer. Then extend the cell range by moving the cell pointer to the last cell in the range. The range of cells that you wish to copy into should now be *highlighted*. Press ENTER to confirm.

Note: Lotus 1-2-3 displays a double full stop to separate addresses in a range though you may only type one.

If you anchor the cell pointer in the wrong cell press ESC to unanchor it. Move to the start (or end) of the range and type **.** (full stop) to anchor it again. You can then use the cursor keys to highlight your range and press ENTER.

Activity 7.1 Copying using the mouse

1   TYPE in any three numbers into cells A1, B1, C1.

2   CLICK in cell **A1**.

3   MOVE the cursor to the control panel.

4   CLICK **Copy**.

5   DRAG **A1..C1**.

6   CLICK to set the range.

7   CLICK **A5**. The cell reference (A5) of the target range is displayed after the 'To where?' prompt.

8   CLICK to confirm.

Your three numbers will be copied into A5, B5 and C5.

Absolute, relative and mixed copying

Before copying formulae, be sure you understand these terms.

Relative addressing

1-2-3's default cell reference type is relative. This means that if a formula is copied or moved to a new location any cell addresses it contains are automatically adjusted to the new cell location. Activity 7.2 shows an example of this.

Activity 7.2 Relative copying

1   TYPE in any numbers into cells B5 to E5 and B6 to E6.

2   MOVE the cell pointer to **B7** and TYPE **+B5+B6** and PRESS ENTER (this adds the contents of B5 and B6 and displays the result in B7).

Now copy this formula into cells C7, D7 and E7:

3   SELECT **/C**(opy).

4   At the prompt: **Copy what?** PRESS ENTER to accept **B7**.
    To where? MOVE to **C7** and anchor the range with a **.** (full stop).

5   PRESS RIGHT ARROW to highlight cells **C7**, **D7**, **E7** and PRESS ENTER.

6   MOVE the cell pointer along row 7 and note the changes in formula in the control panel.

Absolute addressing

If, however, the reference to a specific cell needs to be kept an absolute address is necessary. In 1-2-3 this is done by using the **$** sign which ensures that the cell address does not change. Hence **+$B$7** indicates a permanent link to the value of column B row 7 wherever you copy it to.

Mixed addressing

It is possible to have a mixture of relative and absolute addressing. Hence **+$B7** indicates that the column reference should remain the same but the rows should change; **+B$7** would fix the row, while the column is relative and would be updated.

Activity 7.3 Mixed copying

1   SELECT **/ W**(orksheet) **E**(rase) **Y**(es) to clear your work from the screen.

The following example calculates three different interest rate payments for each of three different investment sums.

2　In A1 TYPE **INTEREST RATE CALCULATION**.

3　In B2 TYPE **0.1**.

4　In C2 TYPE **0.12**.

5　In D2 TYPE **0.14**.

6　SELECT **/ R**(ange) **F**(ormat) **P**(ercent) **0** (no decimal places) and PRESS ENTER.

7　PRESS LEFT ARROW key twice to highlight the range B2..D2 then PRESS ENTER.

You now have these figures in percentage form. *See Section C for more details of format options.*

8　In A4 TYPE **10000** PRESS DOWN ARROW .

9　In A5 TYPE **30000** PRESS DOWN ARROW .

10　In A6 TYPE **50000** ENTER .

11　MOVE to B4 and TYPE **+$A4*B$2** PRESS ENTER and 1000 should appear (i.e. 10% of £10000).

Now copy this formula into the other cells.

12　With the pointer in B4: SELECT **/ C**(opy).

1-2-3 prompts: **Copy what? B4..B4**

13　PRESS ENTER to accept this.

1-2-3 prompts: **To where?**

14　PRESS **.** (full stop) to anchor the pointer in B4.

15　PRESS RIGHT ARROW twice to D4.

16　PRESS DOWN ARROW twice to D6.

The range B4..D6 should now be highlighted.

17　PRESS ENTER to accept this.

All the calculations will appear on your spreadsheet. Check the formulae in the cells and see how 1-2-3 has adjusted them. Your spreadsheet should look like the following. The contents of each cell are shown below it.

	A	B	C	D	E	F	G	H
1	INTEREST RATE CALCULATION							
2		10%	12%	14%				
3								
4	10000	1000	1200	1400				
5	30000	3000	3600	4200				
6	50000	5000	6000	7000				
7								
8								
9								
10								
11								
12								
13								
14								
15								
16								
17								
18								
19								
20								

INTEREST.WK1

The following entries were made:

```
A1:  'INTEREST RATE CALCULATION
B2:  (P0) 0.1
C2:  (P0) 0.12
D2:  (P0) 0.14
A4:  10000
B4:  +$A4*B$2
C4:  +$A4*C$2
D4:  +$A4*D$2
A5:  30000
B5:  +$A5*B$2
C5:  +$A5*C$2
D5:  +$A5*D$2
A6:  50000
B6:  +$A6*B$2
C6:  +$A6*C$2
D6:  +$A6*D$2
```

Transposing
If you have any data set out columnwise and would like it rearranged rowwise (or vice versa) use **Range Transpose** and respond to prompts as in the Copy command.

Activity 7.4 Transposing

1   ENTER any four numbers into cells D7, D8, D9 and D10.

2   With the pointer in D7: SELECT **/ R**(ange) **T**(rans).

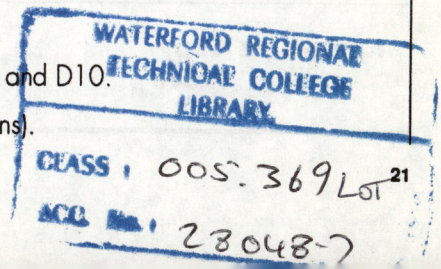

21

1-2-3 prompts: **Transpose what?**

3   HIGHLIGHT **D7..D9** ENTER. This is the part of the column that you wish to transpose.

1-2-3 prompts: **To where?**

4   MOVE to **E15** - the first cell where you want the data to appear as a row.

5   PRESS ENTER.

The cell contents are erased from column D and moved to row 15, (E15..H15).

Activity 7.5 Moving

The **Move** command may be used to move a range of cells from one part of the worksheet to another. It works in the same way as the **Copy** command with 1-2-3 prompting for **Move what?** and **To where?** ranges. Try moving the work you have just created.

1   PRESS the HOME key to MOVE to **A1**.

2   SELECT **/ M**(ove).

1-2-3 prompts: **Move what?**

3   PRESS RIGHT ARROW 3 times to D1.

4   PRESS DOWN ARROW 5 times to D6.

The range A1..D6 should now be highlighted.

5   PRESS ENTER to accept this.

1-2-3 prompts: **To where?**

6   PRESS DOWN ARROW down to A10 and PRESS ENTER.

This moves the block down to the range starting at cell A10. 1-2-3 remembers the shape and size of the range so you only need to tell it the top left corner of the new location (in this case A10). Move the pointer around the range and note how the formulae have been adjusted to reflect their new locations. Keep practising the **Copy** and **Move** features.

Key words	Copy	Absolute	Mixed
	Move	Retrieve	Transpose

Task 8   **A worked example of a spreadsheet**

Objectives   To learn how to:

- widen a column
- copy data and formula
- use the @SUM function
- justify a range of labels
- insert or delete a row or column
- use the repeat key

Instructions   This task takes you through the process of setting up a 'real' spreadsheet and covers a number of different features which appear elsewhere in the *Guide*. Its main aim is for you to revise some of the work that you have done so far while also learning some new skills. You should now be able to create the following spreadsheet.

```
A:A1: [W13]                                                          READY

     A              B         C          D          E          F          G
1                         SUE,GRABBIT and RUN
2
3                   Q1        Q2         Q3         Q4        YEAR
4
5   Sales income  100000    120000     150000     170000     540000
6   Cost of sales  60000     70000      90000     100000     320000
7                 ----------------------------------------------------
8   Gross Profit   40000     50000      60000      70000     220000
9   Overheads      15000     18000      22500      25500      81000
10                ----------------------------------------------------
11  Net Profit     25000     32000      37500      44500     139000
12                ====================================================
13
14
15
16
17
18
19
20
SGR.WK1
```

Clearly, the text and some of the figures will have to be typed in, but if the spreadsheet is to have any advantages over the word processor, you should be able to do better than to type the lot in!

Activity 8.1 Data Entry

1   If you have continued from the previous Task use **/ W**(orksheet) **E**(rase) **Y**(es) to clear the screen. TYPE in the company name heading e.g. **Sue, Grabbit and Run** *or* your name will do.

2   TYPE in all the labels (the text bits), putting **Q1** into B3, **Q2** into C3 etc. In A5 ENTER **Sales Income** then move down and ENTER the other labels - **Cost of sales** in A6, **Gross Profit** in A7 etc - IGNORE *the dotted lines for now and do not leave blank lines.* (You will create them in Activity 8.6).

3   In rows 5 and 6, ENTER the eight sales and cost figures (not the annual totals!)

Note: some of the text in column A is chopped off when you enter figures in B5 and B6. This is because the standard column width is only 9 characters.

Activity 8.2 Widening a column

1   In column A, PRESS **/ W**(orksheet) **C**(olumn) **S**(et-width) and PRESS RIGHT ARROW until all the text reappears in the cell. PRESS ENTER.
Note: [W13] appears in the control panel. Instead of using the ARROW keys you could have typed the column width that you require - **13** in this case.

Mouse users POINT to the intersection between colimns A and B and DRAG to the required width.

Activity 8.3 Copying

Given that the overheads are 15% of sales, all of the remaining empty cells can be filled in by calculation i.e. by 1-2-3 itself. You simply have to tell it what the calculations are. For example, Gross Profit for Quarter 1 (Q1) is Sales less Costs.

1   TYPE **+B5-B6** into **B7**.

For the other quarters you can copy this formula across.

2   With the cell pointer in B7 PRESS **/C**(opy).

The control panel will show the message: **Copy what? B7..B7**.

3   This is the cell we wish to copy so PRESS ENTER.

The message now reads: **To where? B7**.

4   TYPE **C7..E7** (i.e. Q2 to Q4 Gross Profits) and PRESS ENTER .

5   Overheads are 15% of sales so with the cell pointer in B8: TYPE **+B5*0.15** ENTER

Now COPY this formula into C8, D8 and E8. This time copy by pointing rather than typing.

6   With the cell pointer in B8 PRESS **/ C**(opy). Read and accept the control panel message by hitting ENTER .

ENTER the range to copy to:

7   MOVE the cell pointer to cell **C8** using RIGHT ARROW .

8   TYPE **.** (full stop).

9   PRESS RIGHT ARROW twice.

Cells C8 to E8 should be highlighted. The control panel will confirm the target range.

10 To accept PRESS ENTER .

This is a good way of copying small ranges of data as you can see what you are getting. Remember that you can use a mouse to point.

11 Work out the Net Profit for Q1 and COPY it accross as above.

12 In cell B9 ENTER **+B7-B8**.

13 SELECT **/ C**(opy)
    Copy what? B9. PRESS ENTER to accept.
    To where? TYPE **C9..E9**, and PRESS ENTER to complete the operation.

Activity 8.4 The @SUM Function

Year totals are best done using one of 1-2-3's many in-built *functions*. @SUM(list) calculates the total of all cells in a list (specified range).

1   In cell F5 TYPE **@SUM(B5..E5)** and PRESS ENTER . This saves typing +B5+C5 etc.

2   COPY this formula downwards this time into F6..F9.

Note: After the opening bracket has been entered i.e. @SUM(you can POINT to the required range using cursors or mouse.

Now for some tidying up. Numbers are always right aligned and cannot be changed. Labels (text) are initially left aligned but can be set to the left or right edge of the cell or centred. The quarterly labels Q1 etc are all left justified and would look better if they were right aligned with the numbers.

Activity 8.5 Label alignment

1   MOVE to B3 and PRESS / **R**(ange) **L**(abel) **R**(ight).

2   Use the RIGHT ARROW key to highlight all of your labels in row **3** i.e. B3 to F3. PRESS ENTER.

Activity 8.6 Inserting and deleting columns and rows

Finally, to insert the dotted lines.

1   MOVE to row **7** and PRESS / **W**(orksheet) **I**(nsert) **R**(ow) and PRESS ENTER.

2   MOVE to **B7** and TYPE **\-** (back slash key followed by a dash) ENTER.

The *repeat* (****) key fills the cell with the chosen character.

3   COPY B7 across to F7 in the usual way. Insert new rows and create the other two dotted lines as above. **\=** will give the double-dotted line effect on the last line.

You can insert a new column in much the same way.

4   Position your cell pointer in column B:PRESS / **W**(orksheet) **I**(nsert) **C**(olumn) ENTER.

A new column B will appear. Now delete it for practice.

5   PRESS / **W**(orksheet) **D**(elete) **C**(olumn) ENTER.

Finally save your work.

6   SELECT / **F**(ile) **S**(ave) and name it **SGR**.

Your spreadsheet should appear as follows.

```
A:A1: [W13]                                                              READY

    A           A              B         C         D         E         F         G
1                              SUE,GRABBIT and RUN
2
3                             Q1        Q2        Q3        Q4       YEAR
4
5    Sales income         100000    120000    150000    170000    540000
6    Cost of sales         60000     70000     90000    100000    320000
7                        ------------------------------------------------
8    Gross Profit          40000     50000     60000     70000    220000
9    Overheads             15000     18000     22500     25500     81000
10                       ------------------------------------------------
11   Net Profit            25000     32000     37500     44500    139000
12                       ================================================
13
14
15
16
17
18
19
20
SGR.WK1
```

Mouse users: Icons to Insert/Delete column(s)/row(s) are on Palette 3.

Key words	Copy
	@Sum
	Repeat
	Insert column/row
	Delete column/row

Task 9   **Ranges**

Objectives   To understand the concept of ranges.
                   To erase a range and create a named range.
                   To use search and replace within a range.

Instructions   A **range** can be a single cell or any rectangular block of linked cells. You can tell 1-2-3
                   what data you want to work with by specifying or naming the range.

                   The following diagram shows a number of ranges.

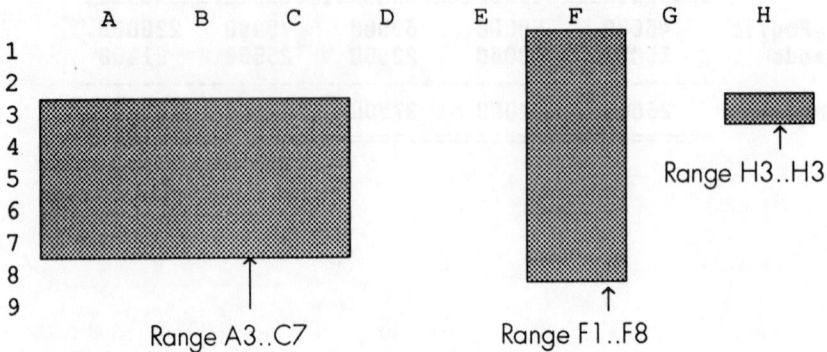

Range A3..C7   Range F1..F8   Range H3..H3

Specifying a range
Many 1-2-3 commands require you to specify a range. You can specify a range before
or after you select a command. Pre-selecting a range is useful when you want to perform
more than one task in relation to it.

To specify a range you need to indicate the top left and bottom right cell address of the
range. The range addresses in the diagram are:

A3..C7
F1..F8
H3

Non-contiguous ranges (i.e. not in adjacent columns or rows) can also be handled
by 1-2-3. e.g. **@SUM(A3..C7,F1..F8)** would sum all the values in these 2 ranges.

Activity 9.1 Naming ranges

1   SELECT **/ F**(ile) **R**(etrieve) **SGR** to call up the Sue, Grabbit and Run file (or the name
    that you gave the file in Activity 8.6).

You are going to change the quarterly labels and YEAR label and align them.

2   Goto to cell **B3**.

3   PRESS F4 (function key F4).

4   HIGHLIGHT **B3..F3** with the RIGHT ARROW key and PRESS ENTER.

This range is now pre-selected for you to use.

5   SELECT **/ R**(ange) **E**(rase) to erase the existing labels.

Mouse users: SELECT B3..F3 by clicking and dragging. CLICK **Erase** icon.

6   In B3 TYPE **Jan** (PRESS RIGHT ARROW after each entry to MOVE to the next cell).

7   In C3 TYPE **Feb**.

8   In D3 TYPE **March**.

9   In E3 TYPE **April**.

10   In F3 TYPE **YTD** (i.e. Year To Date).

Activity 9.2 Naming ranges

Naming a range of cells makes life much easier when you want to refer to a range in a command or formula.

1   SELECT **/ R**(ange) **N**(ame) **C**(reate).

1-2-3 will prompt: **Enter name:**

2   TYPE **DATES** and PRESS ENTER.

1-2-3 will prompt: **Enter Range:**

3   HIGHLIGHT **B3..F3** with the ARROW key and PRESS ENTER. You should be in F3. This does not matter. You can PRESS the LEFT ARROW to B4 to give you the same range. However, if the cell pointer is ever anchored in the wrong range PRESS ESC to unanchor it.

4   MOVE to the start (or end) of the range and TYPE **.** (full stop) to anchor it again. You can then use the pointer keys to highlight the cell range and PRESS ENTER.

Although nothing has changed on screen you now have a range called DATES which covers cells B3..F3. You can use this name with *any* command that prompts for a range. Names should be quicker to use and easier to remember than cell references. For example:

5   SELECT **/ R**(ange) **L**(abel) **R**(ight).

1-2-3 will prompt: **Enter range of labels:**

6   TYPE **DATES** (upper or lower case will do) and PRESS ENTER.

All of the labels in the pre-selected range B3..F3 should now be right aligned. Remember to PRESS ESC if you need to cancel a pre-selected range.

Activity 9.3 Specifying a range after selecting a command

1   MOVE to **D3**.

2   SELECT **/ R**(ange) **L**(abel) **C**(entre).

1-2-3 prompts: **Enter range of labels: D3..D3** because you have de-selected the range, you must specify the range again as follows:

3   PRESS ESC to unanchor the cell pointer.

4   PRESS the LEFT ARROW twice and move to the start of the range **B3**.

5   PRESS **.** (full stop) to anchor it again.

6   PRESS RIGHT ARROW to highlight the cell range **B3..F3** and PRESS ENTER. The labels are now centred. Keep practising this.

Activity 9.4 Range search

Range search finds or replaces a specified string in a range and is very useful in large spreadsheets.

1   SELECT **/ R**(ange) **S**(earch).

1-2-3 prompts: **ENTER range to search:**

2   HIGHLIGHT or TYPE **A1..F12**.

Lotus prompts: **ENTER string to search for:**

3   TYPE **Profit** ENTER.

4   SELECT **L**(abels) **R**(eplace).

1-2-3 prompts: **ENTER replacement string:**

5   TYPE **LOOT** ENTER.

6   SELECT **A**(ll) and note the change to the two labels in A8 and A11.

7   PRESS ALT-F4 to **Undo** the last command and restore the correct labels. SAVE your

file and call it **SGR2** (*or* choose another name). You will TYPE the filename as it is new.

Note: Undo cancels the latest change to your worksheet, restoring the previous data or format. (*See* Activity 6.2).

Key words Range
            Name
            Search
            Replace

Task 10   **Entering statistics**

Objectives   To set up a worksheet involving some of 1-2-3's statistical functions.
To revise tasks learnt so far.

Instructions   Look at the following illustration of the CARS worksheet.

	A	B	C	D	E	F
1	filename CARS		Arthur Daley motors			
2			Car Sales for August 19-9			
3						
4		Basic	Special	GTX	Turbo	Deluxe
5						
6	Basic Price	5995.00	6995.00	9995.00	10995.00	15495,00
7	VAT	1049.13	1224.13	1749.13	1924.13	2711.63
8	Price inc tax	7044.13	8219.13	11744.13	12919.13	18206.63
9	Number plates	25.00	25.00	25.00	25.00	25.00
10	Price on road	7069.13	8244.13	11769.13	12944.13	18231.63
11						
12	Monthly sales	7	10	6	8	2
13	Total sales	49483.88	82441.25	70614.75	103553.00	36463.25
14						
15						
16	Grand Total	342556.13				
17						
18	Average price	10380.49				
19	Number of models	5				
20	Best seller (value)	103553.00				
21	Worst seller (value)	36463.25				

The aim of this Task is to recreate it. Think about how to lay out the information and, in particular which of the figures are **derived** i.e. those that you can get 1-2-3 to work out for you.

Activity 10.1 Entering labels and values

1   MOVE the pointer to C1.

2   TYPE **Arthur Daley Motors** and PRESS ENTER.

3   MOVE to **C2** and TYPE **Car sales for August 19-9**.

Remember to use the BACKSPACE key for deleting a character while creating a cell entry or, once entered, the edit key F2 for changing contents.

4
In cell:	TYPE:	PRESS:
B4	**"Basic**	RIGHT ARROW
C4	**"Special**	RIGHT ARROW
D4	**"GTX**	RIGHT ARROW
E4	**"Turbo**	RIGHT ARROW
F4	**"Deluxe**	ENTER

5   PRESS F5 (the Goto key) and TYPE **A6** PRESS ENTER.

6 Then TYPE in the remaining text down the left hand column as follows:

In cell:	TYPE:	PRESS:
A6	**Basic Price**	DOWN ARROW
A7	**VAT**	DOWN ARROW
A8	**Price inc tax**	DOWN ARROW
A9	**Number plates**	DOWN ARROW
A10	**Price on road**	DOWN ARROW (x2)
A12	**Monthly sales**	DOWN ARROW
A13	**Total sales**	DOWN ARROW (x3)
A16	**Grand Total**	DOWN ARROW (x2)
A18	**Average price**	DOWN ARROW
A19	**Number of models**	DOWN ARROW
A20	**Best seller (value)**	DOWN ARROW
A21	**Worst seller (value)**	DOWN ARROW

Having entered these details you will notice that column A will not be wide enough if you are to enter figures into column B.

7 To widen the column TYPE **/** (to call up the commands) and then **ENTER** the following sequence (point to menu item or press 1st letter):

WCS (**W**orksheet, **C**olumn, **S**et-width) and then use the RIGHT ARROW key to widen the column (20 characters will do). PRESS ENTER to confirm.

8 PRESS F5. TYPE **B6** and ENTER.

9 ENTER the basic prices of the cars as whole numbers in cells B6 to F6 (see the CARS worksheet at the start of the Task for details).

Activity 10.2 Change figures to two decimal places

Now change all the figures to two decimal places so that you can deal in money.

1 ENTER the following command sequence:

/WGFF (**W**orksheet, **G**lobal, **F**ormat, **F**ixed) and PRESS ENTER to accept the default of 2 places.

2 PRESS Goto F5; TYPE **B7** ENTER.

3 In **B7** TYPE in this formula:
    +B6*17.5% (i.e. VAT is 17.5% of basic price)

4 Now copy this formula across. PRESS **/C**(opy).

5 The control panel will prompt: **Copy what? B7..B7**. To accept this PRESS ENTER.

6 The **Copy to where?** prompt appears. To move to the start of the target range

(i.e. C7) PRESS RIGHT ARROW.

7   Anchor this cell by PRESSING **.** (full stop). Now PRESS RIGHT ARROW three
    times to cover (highlight) the area that you want to copy to i.e. **C7..F7**.

8   PRESS ENTER.

The VAT figures should now appear. MOVE the cursor along row 7 and look at each
formula in the control panel (top left of display screen). You will see that 1-2-3 has
adjusted the formula according to its relative position on the worksheet. **Relative
copying** was introduced in Task 7.

9   MOVE to B8 and TYPE **+B6+B7**.

10 COPY this across to C8..F8.

11 In B9 TYPE **25** and COPY that into C9..F9.

12 In B10 TYPE **+B8+B9** and COPY this along to C10..F10.

The top part of your spreadsheet should now be complete - check it with the worksheet
at the start of this Task. Well done if it agrees; if not go back and check your work.

Activity 10.3 Completing the spreadsheet

1   TYPE the monthly sales figures into cells B12 to F12.

You have just set all your figures to two decimal places but you are selling whole cars.
You therefore need a range command.

2   PRESS **/RFF** (**R**ange, **F**ormat, **F**ixed) and TYPE **0** for the number of decimal places.

3   PRESS ENTER and the message: **Enter range to format** will appear.

4   TYPE (or point) **B12..F12** ENTER . Your figures in this range should now be whole
    numbers.

5   In B13 TYPE **+B10*B12** ENTER and COPY across.

6   When you see a row of asterisks, 1-2-3 is telling you that it has a figure that will not
    quite fit so WIDEN the column to 10 characters wide.

In B16 you need to enter the sum of B13 to F13. You can TYPE **+B13+B14** etc but
there is a quicker way and that is by using one of the many functions available in 1-2-3.

7   In B16 TYPE **@SUM(B13..F13)**, ENTER.

8   In B18 TYPE **+B16/@SUM(B12..F12)**, ENTER. This formula will divide total sales
    by the number of cars to find the average selling price.

9   In B19 TYPE **@COUNT(B4..F4)**, ENTER. This function counts the number of types
    of cars sold i.e. 5. Reformat the cell to show a whole number.

10 In B20 TYPE **@MAX(B13..F13)**, ENTER. This should pick up the maximum sales value in row 13.

11 Similarly in B21 TYPE **@MIN(B13..F13)** This should give you the minimum value from the same range.

Obviously these functions are more useful when you have more figures to search for but these should give you the idea.

12 Now SAVE this worksheet - **/FS** (**F**ile **S**ave) with the file name **CARS**.

Key words   F2 (Edit)
            F5 (Goto)
            @SUM
            @COUNT
            @MAX
            @MIN

Task 11   Printing your worksheet

Objective   To print out your worksheet.

Instructions   It is useful to print out your worksheet so that you have a hard copy. Use the 1-2-3 print commands when you need a quick printout. You see in a later task how *Wysiwyg* can enhance the look of your output.

Print out the CARS worksheet you saved at the end of Task 10.

SELECT **/FR CARS** if it is not current.

/ P(rint) commands let you create printed copies of a worksheet. Always check that your printer is properly set up and switched on with the paper correctly aligned. You may have to run the INSTALL program again to set up the correct printer drivers.

Activity 11.1   Printing your worksheet

1   SELECT **/ P**(rint) **P**(rinter) **R**(ange) then TYPE (or point) **A1..F21**.

2   Check the paper and printer status. Make sure that the print head is at the top of a new sheet of paper.

3   SELECT **A**(lign) to tell 1-2-3 that the paper is in position.

4   SELECT **G**(o) to start printing.

5   When the printing has finished, SELECT **P**(age) to advance the paper to the top of the next sheet.

6   SELECT **Q**(uit).

Print options

There are many print options including the ability to:

- insert headers and footers at the top and bottom of each page
- set margins - left, right, top or bottom
- set borders to print column and row references
- set up printer strings - to specify font size and style of print e.g. **\015** will give compressed print
- determine page length by specifying the number of lines per page
- print as displayed or the underlying cell formulae, formatted or unformatted

---

Activity 11.2   Printing a worksheet with a header, footer and page number

1   SELECT **/ P**(rint) **P**(rinter).]The **Print settings** dialog box appears.

36

Note: the range has already been defined in the last activity. It is useful to use the **dialog box** when several settings need to be changed at once.

2   PRESS F2 to activate the dialog box.

3   TYPE **H** to select **Header** to place text at the top of each page.

4   TYPE **Monthly Accounts Page # @** and PRESS ENTER

This entry tells 1-2-3 to print "Monthly Accounts" to the left margin, page number in the middle and the date to the right. The split vertical bars position the header in different places on the line. 1-2-3 replaces the # (hash) with the page number when you print and **@** with today's date.

5   TYPE **F** for **footer** to put text at the bottom of each page.

6   TYPE **A. Daley confidential report.**

7   PRESS ENTER

8   PRESS ENTER to SELECT **OK**.

9   SELECT **G**(o) to print out. 1-2-3 will print out the header, page 1 and the print range but not the footer.

Monthly Accounts

	A	B	C	D	E	F
1	filename CARS		Arthur Daley Motors			
2			Car sales for August 19-9			
3						
4		Basic	Special	GTX	Turbo	Deluxe
5						
6	Basic Price	5995.00	6995.00	9995.00	10995.00	15495.00
7	VAT	1049.13	1224.13	1749.13	1924.13	2711.63
8	Price inc tax	7044.13	8219.13	11744.13	12919.13	18206.63
9	Number plates	25.00	25.00	25.00	25.00	25.00
10	Price on road	7069.13	8244.13	11769.13	12944.13	18231.63
11						
12	Monthly sales	7	10	6	8	2
13	Total sales	49483.88	82441.25	70614.75	103553.00	36463.25
14						
15						
16	Grand Total	342556.13				
17						
18	Average price	10380.49				
19	Number of models	5				
20	Best seller (value)	103553.00				
21	Worst seller (value)	36463.25				

A. Daley confidential report

To print the footer:

10 SELECT **P**(age) to advance to the next page.

11 SELECT **Q**(uit).

12 SELECT **/ F**(ile) **S**(ave) **CARS**.

Print destinations

Rather than printing straight away it is possible to save print files to disk. A **Print file** contains data, including text and printer options e.g. headers but no graphs or special printer codes. It can be printed out later from DOS or used in other programs such as word processing ones.

To **save** a print file you simply need to:

SELECT **/ P**(rint) **F**(ile) and type the filename.

Print output can also be sent to an **Encoded file**. This file saves not just your data but all of your graphs, the print settings and printer codes that you have given. It is useful to use an encoded file if you want to print on a printer that is not connected to your computer. To do this:

SELECT **/ P**(rint) **E**(ncoded) and type the filename for this routine.

It is also possible to send print output to an encoded file and then print it in the **background** i.e. while you get on with another Task. This saves time if you need to print out very large files.

To do this:

SELECT **/ Q**(uit) to leave 1-2-3 (remembering to save your file if you need to).

TYPE **bprint** at the C: \123R24 operating system prompt. You can then re-enter 1-2-3 and SELECT **/ P**(rint) **B**(ackground) to use background printing. Refer to the 1-2-3 **user guide** for more information on **BPrint**.

You will return to printing in Task 36 using 1-2-3's publishing add-in *Wysiwyg*.

Key words **Print**
Header
Footer
Page
Encoded file
BPrint
Background

Section C: Settings and formatting ▬▬▬▬▬

Task 12   **Changing global settings**

Objective   To change the date-time indicator.

Instructions   The date-and-time indicator appears on the status line bottom-left of your screen. It is possible to change this to show the name of the file that you are working on. This is useful when you have a large number of files.

Activity 12.1 The clock

1   SELECT **/ F**(ile) **R**(etrieve) **SGR** to recall the SGR file.

2   SELECT **/ W**(orksheet) **G**(lobal). The **Global Settings** dialog box appears.

3   SELECT **Default**. The Default Settings dialog box appears. Note that the clock display setting is standard (top right of sheet).

4   PRESS F2 .

5   SELECT **C**(lock) **F**(ilename).

Note: The clock display setting now has an asterisk marking File name and the status line at the bottom of the screen shows SGR.WK1.

6   SELECT **U**(pdate) **Q**(uit) to save the new setting and return to *ready* mode.

For practise change back to the date-and-time:

7   SELECT **/WGDOCCUQ** (just the first letters of the commands are shown here.)

Activity 12.2 Global settings

There are other useful **/ W**(orksheet) **G**(lobal) settings commands which you should experiment with.

1   SELECT **/W**(orksheet) **G**(lobal) **D**(efault) **O**(ther) **B**(eep) to turn the computer's bell on or off when an error occurs.

2   SELECT **/WGDO I**(nternational) **N**(egative) to show either brackets or a minus sign with negative numbers. You will try this in Task 10.

Key words Date-and-time indicator

Task 13   **Formatting the worksheet**

Objectives   To show how changes can be made to the appearance of the worksheet and how data is displayed.

Instructions   **Changing cell formats**

You have seen how 1-2-3 enables you to:

- change the way figures (*values*) are displayed
- change the width of columns
- change the position of a label in a cell
- insert a row (or column).

You will practise more formatting in the next two tasks.

1-2-3 lets you display data in cells in a number of ways. You can use one format for the whole spreadsheet with **/W**(orksheet) **G**(lobal) **F**(ormat) or several different ones using **/ R**(ange) **F**(ormat).

Activity 13.1 Formatting

1   SELECT **/FR** and retrieve the **SGR2** file (saved at the end of Task 9).

You are now going to display all of the numbers with two decimal places.

2   SELECT **/WGFF**(ixed).

1-2-3 will prompt: **ENTER the number of decimal places (0..15):2**.

3   PRESS ENTER to accept **2** (the default number).

Asterisks may be shown in cells which are not wide enough to display this format.
To change the width of all the columns:

4   SELECT **/ W**(orksheet) **G**(lobal) **C**(olumn-width).

1-2-3 prompts to **Enter global column width (1..240)**:

5   PRESS RIGHT ARROW to increase width to **10**.
6   PRESS ENTER to accept this.

Reset the format to Currency showing £ signs and commas.

7   SELECT **/WGFC**(urrency) **2** ENTER.
8   Again increase the column width if necessary to 12 so that the data is displayed.

40

To display the Net profit figures in currency as whole numbers:

9   SELECT **/ R**(ange) **F**(ormat) **C**(urrency) **0** (i.e. no decimal places).

1-2-3 prompts: **Range to format:**

10 TYPE (or point) **B11..E11** and PRESS⎡ENTER⎤.

You do not need to save this file; just **/ Q**(uit) **Y**(es) **Y**(es) when you have finished.

Key words	Currency
	Range
	Format
	Global
	Fixed

Task 14 Formatting figures

Objectives   To format and present figures.
To freeze titles on screen.

Instructions   **Presentation of figures**.

Input
Apart from simple numbers you may end a number with a % sign and 1-2-3 will store the entry after dividing it by 100. Thus 15% is stored as 0.15. You can also enter numbers in scientific notation e.g. 1,234,000 as 1.234E+06 (exponential).

Output
You learnt in Task 13 that there are two command sequences for output formats, i.e. **/ W**(orksheet) **G**(lobal) **F**(ormat) which lets you set a format for all the cells and **/ R**(ange) **F**(ormat) which controls the display in specified ranges.

Either will display the following menu:

Fixed Sci Currency, General +/- Percent Date Text Hidden Reset

Selection allows you to set the form in which the numbers are presented.

Fixed   specifies number of decimal places (0 - 15)
Sci(entific)   number in the form 1.234E+06
Currency   commas to separate thousands, preceeding £ sign and negative values in brackets e.g. (£234,567.10)
Comma (,) commas to separate thousands, negative values in brackets
General   the default format, number usually as input but insignificant zeros to the right of the decimal point are suppressed
+/-   crude bar chart of + or - within cell
Percent   multiplies stored value by 100 and displays it with a % sign
Date   date and time formats
Text   displays formula underlying the number normally shown
Hidden   hides cell contents
Reset   will change specified range of cells to default format

Try these in Activity 14.1 to see the different effects. The right format can give a professional look to a document.

Activity 14.1

1   In cells A2 to A11 TYPE in the labels **FIXED, SCIENTIFIC** etc, as in the spreadsheet shown in Activity 14.2 below. Use **'**(apostrophe) to ensure text when you enter the label **'+/-**.

2   In cells B1 across to F1, TYPE in the numbers **7, @TODAY, 0.000000123, 37.5** and **12345**.

(@TODAY is a built-in function which translates the computer system date into a value which is displayed in the cell (*see* Section E for more information).)

3   Copy the numbers down as follows:

4   MOVE to B1.

5   SELECT **/C**(opy).

6   **Copy what?** HIGHLIGHT *or* TYPE **B1..F1** ⟨ENTER⟩.

7   **To where?** HIGHLIGHT *or* TYPE **B2..F11** ⟨ENTER⟩.

The numbers should fill rows 2 to 11.

Activity 14.2

Now format each of the rows 2 to 11 to match the labels you have just entered.

1   MOVE to B2.

2   SELECT **/RFF2** ⟨ENTER⟩.

3   When prompted **Enter range to format:** PRESS ⟨RIGHT ARROW⟩ 4 times to highlight cells B2..F2 then PRESS ⟨ENTER⟩. This will format row 2 with a fixed format of 2 decimal places.

Now repeat the process for the other rows. Start each row with the cell pointer in column B.

4   TYPE **/RF** followed by the initial letter of the relevant format etc.

Note: for **,** (Comma) PRESS the comma key and for Date choose format 1. (For information on Date *see* Section E, Tasks 19 and 20).

The control panel will display format information, for example, if you move to cell B2, the panel will read B2: (F2) 7. (F2) denotes that the cell is formatted to *fixed* with 2 decimal places.

To widen the columns so that text and figures will be shown:

5   SELECT **/WGC12** ⟨ENTER⟩. This will widen all columns to 12 characters. Some asterisks remain in the +/- row.

The following spreadsheet shows how **7**, **@TODAY**, **0.000000123**, **37.5** and **12345** look in their various formats.

	A	B	C	D	E	F
1		7	33138	0.000000123	37.5	12345
2	FIXED	7.00	33138.00	0.00	37.50	12345.00
3	SCIENTIFIC	7.00E+00	3.31E+04	1.23E-07	3.75E+01	1.23E+04
4	CURRENCY	£7.00	£33,138.00	£0.00	£37.50	£12,345.00
5	COMMA	7.00	33,138.00	0.00	37.50	12,345.00
6	GENERAL	7	33138	0.000000123	37.5	12345
7	+/-	++++++++	**************		**************************	
8	PERCENT	700.00%	3313800.00%	0.00%	3750.00%	1234500.00%
9	DATE	07-Jan-00	22-Sep-90	***********	06-Feb-00	18-Oct-33
10	TEXT	7	33138	0.000000123	37.5	12345
11	HIDDEN					
12						
13						
14						
15						
16						
17						
18						
19						

Activity 14.3 Displaying negative numbers

1 In A12 TYPE **negative** and PRESS ENTER.

2 In B12 TYPE **-123**.

3 SELECT **/ W**(orksheet) **G**(lobal) **D**(efault) **O**(ther) **I**(nternational) **N**(egative) and **P**(arentheses) *or* **S**(ign) to show *either* brackets (parentheses) *or* a minus sign with negative numbers.

Activity 14.4 Representing zero

There are three ways of representing zero in a worksheet - display, blank or label.

1 In cell A13 TYPE **0** ENTER.

Note: 0 is displayed as this is the default.

2 SELECT **/WGZ**(ero) **Y**(es) to blank zero values.

3 SELECT **/WGZ**(ero) **L**(abel).

4 At the prompt **ENTER label:** TYPE **nowt** ENTER. Note the changes to your zero display.

5 Change back to the default setting.

Activity 14.5 Freezing titles on screen

1 MOVE to column **G** and note that you have 'lost' column A on your screen.

It is useful to see your labels so *freeze* them.

2 MOVE to column **B**.

3 SELECT **/ W**(orksheet) **T**(itles) **V**(ertical) to freeze the column to the left of the cell pointer. If you try to move to column A you will not be able to.

4 Now move back to column G. *Note*: the labels in column A stay on screen.

5 SELECT **/ W**(orksheet) **T**(itles) **C**(lear) to *'unfreeze'* column A.

Key words Titles
Freeze

Task 15 Protecting data and files

Objectives   To protect cells from accidental overwriting.
To hide cells from display.
To save a file with a password.

Instructions   It is often sensible to protect or hide all or part of your spreadsheet work. There are many reasons for doing this including confidentiality, the need to prevent changes from being made to the formulae in your model or simply to avoid accidental mistakes. You may also want to hide data so that, for example, two non-adjacent columns of work can be printed out alongside each other.

Activity 15.1 Worksheet (global) protection

PRESS **/ W**(orksheet) **G**(lobal). The **Global Settings** dialog box will appear. This shows you, among other things, whether you can protect your work or not. An x beside *Protection on* denotes that protection is enabled.

If Global protection is disabled and you want to prevent changes in your worksheet:

1   With a new file on screen, SELECT **/ W**(orksheet) **G**(lobal) **P**(rotection) **E**(nable).

Note: **PR** (for protection) will appear in the control panel for every cell in the worksheet.

2   Try typing something in. A pop-up display will appear saying it is a protected cell. PRESS ESC to continue.

3   SELECT **/WGPD**(isable) to turn protection off again.

Activity 15.2 Range protection

More often you will need to protect cells in a given range. For example, assume that cells A1 to F8 are your input area where users can enter figures. Assume also that the rest of your spreadsheet contains various complicated formulae that you want to protect from accidental change or overwriting. Check that global protection is on (enabled).

1   PRESS **/ R**(ange) **U**(nprot).

2   TYPE (or point to) **A1..F8** ENTER.

This will cancel protection and allow change when global protection is on.

3   MOVE the cell pointer anywhere within the range. *Note*: **U**(nprotected cell) appears in line 1 of the control panel for each of these cells.

4   MOVE to the protected area. *Note*: **Pr** (for protected cell) in the control panel.

5   TYPE **'it will not let me in'** ENTER. 1-2-3 will give a beep and the popup box will appear indicating *Error*.

6   PRESS ESC to return to *ready* mode.

Activity 15.3 Hiding data

1   TYPE any nine numbers into A1..C3. Include a **0** among them.

2   SELECT **/ R**(ange) **F**(ormat) **H**(idden) **B1..B3** to hide cells, in this case the range B1 to B3.

3   SELECT **/RFR**(eset) **B1..B3** to restore.

4   With the pointer in cell B1: SELECT **/ W**(orksheet) **C**(olumn) **H**(ide). PRESS ENTER to hide column B.

5   SELECT **/WCD**(isplay) LEFT ARROW ENTER to bring it back.

6   SELECT **/ W**(orksheet) **G**(lobal) **Z**(ero) **Y**(es) to hide all values equal to 0.

Note: **/WGZN** will re-display them.

Activity 15.4 Saving a file with a password

To prevent other users accessing your file you can save it with a password:

1   RETRIEVE any of your worksheet files using **/FR**.

2   PRESS **/ F**(ile) **S**(ave).

3   PRESS the SPACEBAR once. (If the file is new, TYPE in the new filename and then PRESS SPACEBAR.

4   TYPE **P** and then PRESS ENTER.

5   1-2-3 prompts you to **Enter password**.

6   TYPE a password up to 15 letters and PRESS ENTER. Do not forget it.

7   1-2-3 will then ask you to verify password. TYPE it in again.

8   SELECT **R**(eplace) to save your existing file with the password.

9   Now try retrieving the file.

To *change* a password:

10   SELECT **/ F**(ile) **S**(ave).

11   PRESS BACKSPACE to clear the **[PASSWORD PROTECTED]** prompt.

12   PRESS SPACEBAR once and follow procedure from 4 above.

To *delete* a password. Follow points 10 and 11 for changing a password, ignore point

12 and then:

13 PRESS ENTER.

14 SELECT **R**(eplace) to save the file without a password.

Making a backup copy of a file.

It is always sensible to save previous versions of your worksheets. When you SELECT
/ F(ile) **S**(ave) **B**(ackup) 1-2-3 will create a **.BAK** (backup file) of the worksheet stored on
disk before you write over (i.e. update) the current one with your changes.

Key words	**Global**
	Protection
	Enable
	Hide
	Password

Section D: Graphs

Task 16 — Creating graphs

Objective
To create graphs from worksheet data.
To name graphs so that you can work with several at once.
To save graphs for printing.

Instructions
Graphs are excellent ways of displaying data. 1-2-3 offers 7 types of graph:

Line   shows data over time

XY   shows data over time

Bar   compares values side by side

Stack-Bar   compares values on top of each other

Pie   compares parts to a whole

HLCO   tracks the performance of a share

Mixed   combines lines and bars

You must choose the most appropriate one to display your data.

Parts of a graph
You can add titles, labels and legends to a graph. You can change the appearance of a graph by removing the frame, changing the scale or orientation. The following diagram shows the terms used.

49

Graph title ———————— Red Balloon Company (Monthly Sales)

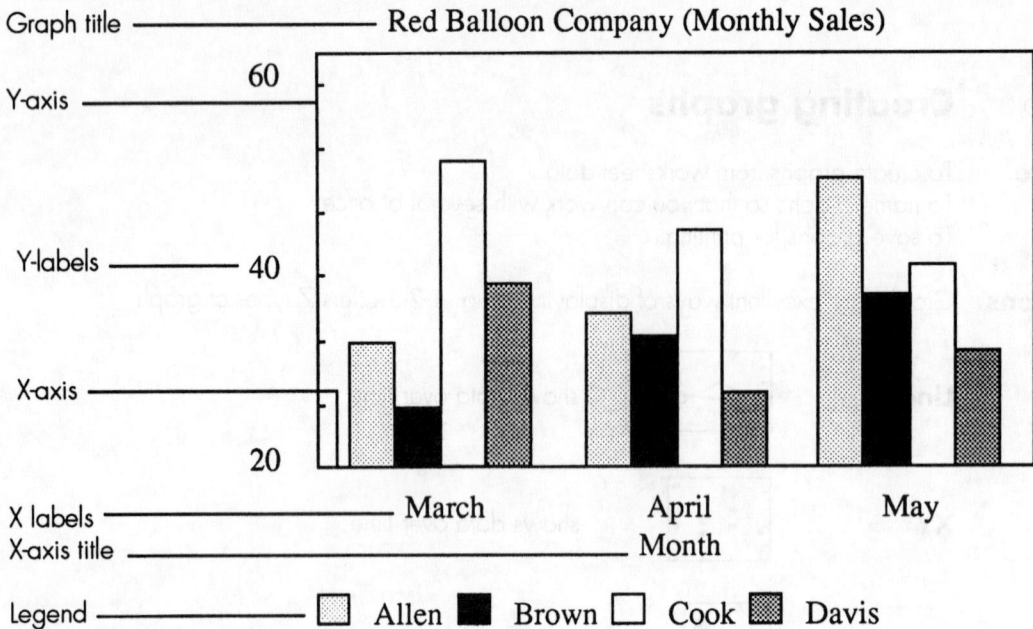

Y-axis ————

60

Y-labels ———————— 40

X-axis ————

20

X labels ———————— March   April   May

X-axis title ———————— Month

Legend ———————— ☐ Allen ■ Brown ☐ Cook ▨ Davis

Use data from the CARS worksheet to create a graph.

Activity 16.1 Creating a bar chart

1 SELECT **/FR CARS** worksheet.

2 SELECT **/ G**(raph) and the **Graph Settings** dialog box will appears. This lists all the settings you can use to draw a graph.

3 PRESS F2 (Edit) to activate the dialog box.

4 SELECT **T**(ype) **B**(ar).

5 SELECT **R**(anges). Then SELECT **A** for the first data range. (You are going to pick the total sales figures so you only need one data range and A is used in these cases).

6 TYPE **B13..F13** ENTER.

7 PRESS ENTER again to accept **OK**.

8 SELECT **View**. You will now see the makings of a picture on screen but you still need to add labels etc to explain what it shows.

9 PRESS ESC to return to the **Graph menu**.

10 Try another way of viewing graphs: PRESS F10 (Graph function key).

11 PRESS F10 again to return to your work.

12 SELECT **O**(ptions) **T**(itles) F2. The **Graph legends** and **Titles box** will appear.

13 SELECT **T**(itles) **F**(irst).

14 TYPE in the first line of your graph title - e.g. **Arthur Daley Motors** ENTER.

Now enter the second line of the graph title:

15 SELECT **T**(itles) **S**(econd) and TYPE **model sales by value** ENTER.

To label the X and Y axes:

16 SELECT **T**(itles) **X**(axis) and TYPE **August 19-9 sales** ENTER.

17 SELECT **T**(itles) **Y**(axis) and TYPE **£**.

18 SELECT **OK** by PRESSING ENTER.

19 PRESS ESC F2 to return to **Graph settings box**.

Now label each of the 5 bar points on the X-axis with the car model names:

20 SELECT **R**(anges) **X**.

21 PRESS F4 to go to your worksheet.

22 TYPE (or point) to the range which covers the five car names - **Basic**, **Special** etc
    i.e. B4..F4.

23 SELECT **OK Q**(uit).

To view your graph:

24 PRESS F10 (graph function key) *or* SELECT **V**(iew).

You can also give the bars a 3-D effect:

25 PRESS ESC (*or* F10 again).

26 SELECT **T**(ype) **F**(eatures) **3**(D-Effect) **Y**(es).

27 PRESS F10 (graph).

Compare it with the graph below to see if the details are correct.

28 PRESS F10 to return to the menu.

Arthur Daley Motors
model sales by value

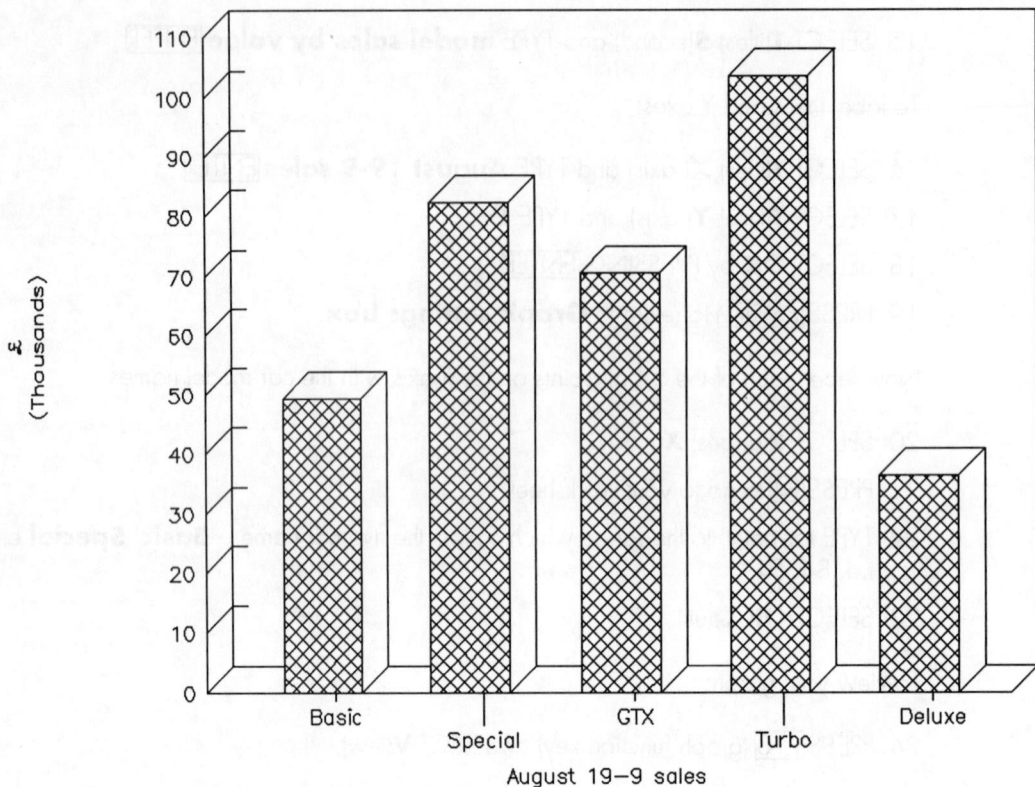

£ (Thousands)

Vertical axis: 0, 10, 20, 30, 40, 50, 60, 70, 80, 90, 100, 110

Bars: Basic, Special, GTX, Turbo, Deluxe

August 19—9 sales

To save more than one graph with a worksheet you must give each graph a name.

29 PRESS ESC ESC.

30 From the graph menu SELECT **N**(ame) **C**(reate).

1-2-3 will prompt **Enter graph name:**

31 TYPE **SALES** ENTER.

This will attach each of the graph settings to the worksheet file. Naming a graph does not save it to disk, so you will need to save your file.

A graph can change to reflect changes in the worksheet data. Go to your worksheet and arbitrarily change a figure (e.g. reduce the sales of GTX to **3**). Now **View** the graph. *Note*: it has automatically changed. Graphs are directly connected to the data that they represent.

Activity 16.2 Saving the graph for printing

1   PRESS ESC to return to the graph menu.

2   SELECT **S**(ave) 1-2-3 will prompt: **Enter graph file name:**

3   TYPE **SALESP** (**P** for print). 1-2-3 saves the graph for printing and attaches a .PIC (picture) suffix to the filename. *Note:* graphs for printing do *not* change to reflect changes in the worksheet. You will need to resave each time you make an amendment to your worksheet file.

4   To save all your work PRESS ESC ESC to get back to the main menu.

5   SELECT **/FS** (and accept file name **CARS**) then **R**(eplace) the original file.

The current worksheet looks just the same but it is now saved with an underlying graph attached to it.

Activity 16.3 Changing the graph type - a pie chart

Using the same data you can create some of the other types of graph quite quickly. Viewing the various options may help to decide on the best one to use, for example, a Pie chart.

1   SELECT **/ G**(raph) **T**(ype) **P**(ie) **V**(iew) and a pie chart will appear.

2   Try out the other types of graph. You can see that the others are not so good for the existing set of data.

Activity 16.4 Shading pie slices

Although the pie chart looks good already, you can improve its appearance further with hatch patterns.

1   PRESS ESC ESC ESC to return to the worksheet.

1-2-3 has seven hatch patterns numbered 1 to 8 (8 is blank).

2   MOVE the pointer to B14 (an empty row)

3   SELECT **/ D**(ata) **F**(ill) 1-2-3 will prompt: **Enter fill range:**

4   TYPE (or point) **B14..F14**

5   **Start: 1** ENTER , **Step: 1** ENTER , **Stop:** ENTER , will accept the default of **8191**.

You have now entered 1 2 3 4 and 5 into cells B14..F14 to use with our pie chart. You could hide these cells with **/ R**(ange) **F**(ormat) **H**(idden) if, for example, you wanted to print the worksheet.

6   SELECT **/ G**(raph) **B** the second data range.

1-2-3 prompts ENTER second data range:
7   TYPE (or point) **B14..F14** ENTER . Now **V**iew the pie chart with hatch patterns.

One further refinement is to explode one or more slices for emphasis. To do this add 100 to the corresponding hatch pattern.

8   PRESS ESC until you get back to your worksheet.

9   MOVE to F14 and TYPE in **105**.

10   SELECT **/ G**(raph) **V**(iew).

The smallest slice has been pulled out (exploded). Your pie should look like this:

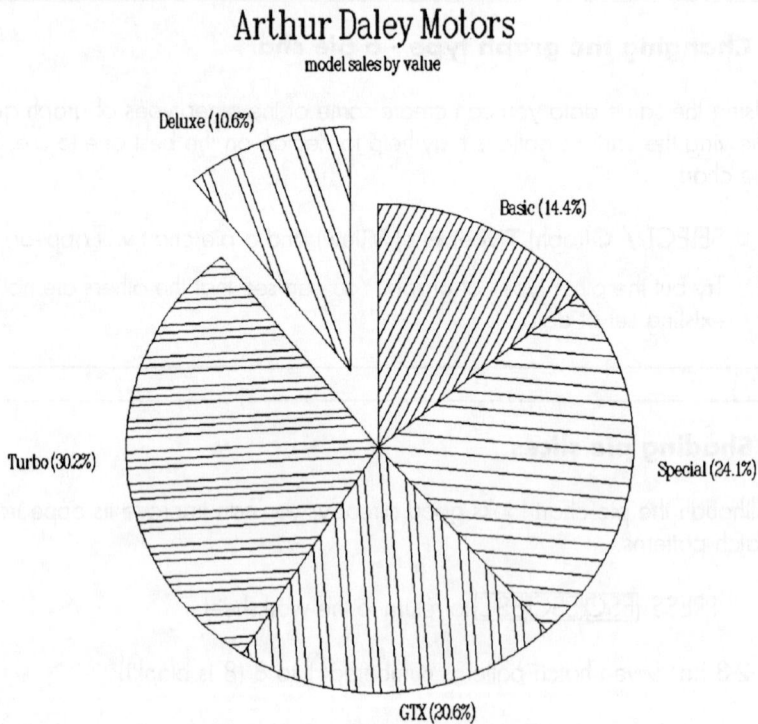

Arthur Daley Motors
model sales by value

Deluxe (10.6%)

Basic (14.4%)

Special (24.1%)

Turbo (30.2%)

GTX (20.6%)

11   PRESS ESC to return to the graph menu.

12   SELECT **N**(ame) **C**(reate) and name the graph **PIE**.

13   SELECT **S**(ave) and name the graph for printing **PIEPRINT**.

14   SELECT **/ F**(ile) **S**(ave) to save your worksheet file with the two named graphs **SALES** and **PIE**.

Activity 16.5 Multiple data ranges

So far you have just used a single data range showing sales figures. Now create a graph showing several data ranges - 1-2-3 allows six. Choose the basic Price, VAT and Price including Tax figures from the CARS worksheet.

1 SELECT **/GT B**(ar).

2 SELECT **G**(roup). This is a quick way of nominating a range of data rather than having to define each row (or column) of data separately in data ranges A, B, C etc.

1-2-3 prompts: **Enter group range:**

3 TYPE (or point) **B4..F8**. This range covers the X data range (the car names) as well as the three rows of figures.

4 PRESS ENTER **R**(owwise) to use the rows as data ranges.

5 SELECT **V**(iew). Price, VAT and Price including Tax are shown in different hatch patterns for each car type.

6 PRESS ESC.

Activity 16.6 Adding legends

1 SELECT **O**(ptions) **L**(egend) **R**(ange).

2 MOVE cell pointer to A5 and highlight A5..A8 ENTER.

3 SELECT **Q**(uit) **V**(iew). The graph now has legends which link the hatch patterns to the data ranges.

4 PRESS ESC.

5 To name the graph, SELECT **NC** and call it **PRICES**.

6 SELECT **S**(ave) file name **PRICESP** to save the graph for printing.

7 SELECT **/FS** filename **CARS** to save the worksheet with three named graphs on disk.

Arthur Daley Motors

model sales by value

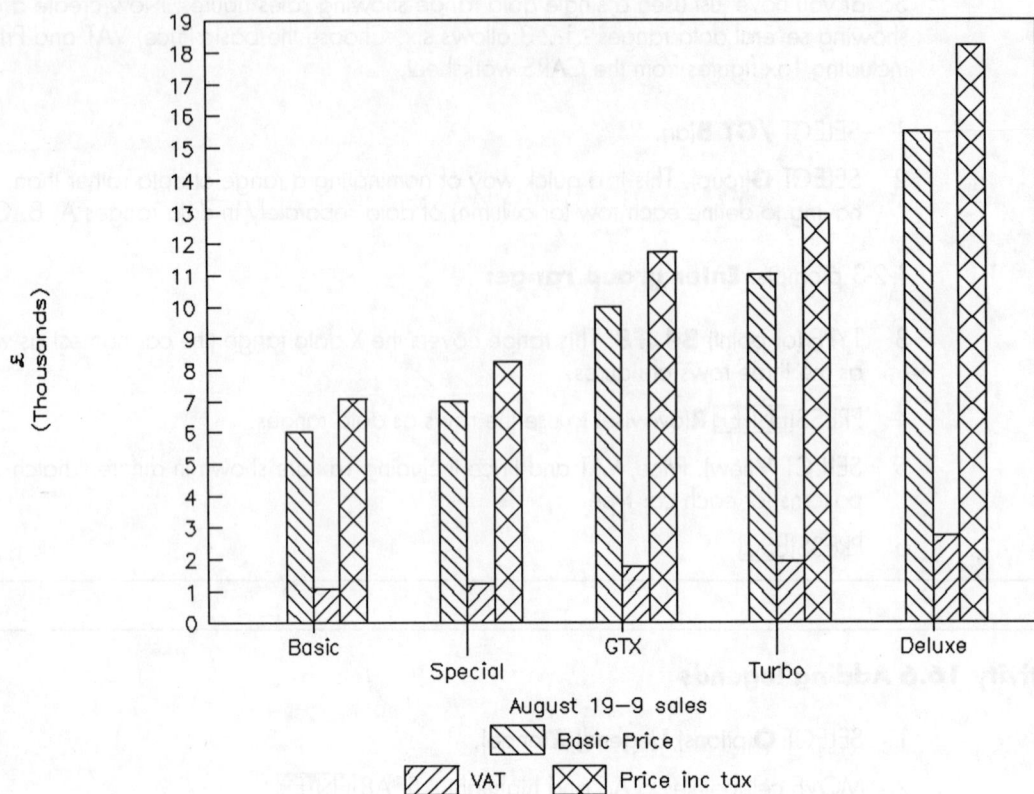

£
(Thousands)

Chart vertical axis: 0 to 19

Categories: Basic, Special, GTX, Turbo, Deluxe

August 19–9 sales

Legend:
- Basic Price
- VAT
- Price inc tax

Key words	Graph	Frame
	Type	Scale
	Legend	Orientation
	Rowwise	Legends
	Titles	Type
	Labels	Features

Task 17   **Printing graphs**

Objective   To print graphs from worksheet data.

Instructions   To save a graph for printing, a special **.PIC** (picture) file has to be created. As 1-2-3 itself does not print graphs, the file will be passed to the *PrintGraph* or *Wysiwyg* programs to be printed out.

Activity 17.1 Print the pie chart in the CARS worksheet

To print the pie chart in the CARS worksheet:

1   SELECT **/FR** if CARS is not currently in use.

2   SELECT **/FLG** (File, List, Graph) to see a list of your .PIC files. You should have SALESP.PIC, PIEPRINT.PIC and PRICESP.PIC saved from the last Task. To print out your graph on paper, leave the 1-2-3 program and start *PrintGraph*.

3   SELECT **/ Q**(uit) **Y**(es).

4   From your Lotus 1-2-3 directory TYPE **lotus** ENTER. This takes you into the **Lotus Access menu**.

5   SELECT **P**(rintGraph).

Note: you can, alternatively, TYPE **pgraph** at the system prompt to go straight to *PrintGraph*. PrintGraph's hardware settings should have been arranged for you but check the following on screen first. Under **Hardware Settings** check that your graphs directory is where you have stored your graph (.PIC) files. If you need to change the setting:

SELECT **S**(ettings) **H**(ardware) **G**(raphs-Directory) and TYPE in the correct location (e.g. **A:** if your graphs are on the A drive floppy disk).

Similarly check your fonts directory. This is where the font (.FNT) files are kept and include the typefaces used to print graphs and text. If you need to change the setting:

SELECT **F**(onts-Directory) (e.g. this would be **C:\123R23** if they were held on a directory called 123R23 on your hard disk).

Also, check the printer setting. When the program was installed several printers may have been specified so:

SELECT **P**(rinter).

Use the ARROW keys to highlight the printer you wish to use then:

PRESS SPACE BAR to mark your selection (a # appears).

PRESS ENTER to accept the printer.

SELECT **Q**(uit) to return to the settings menu.

If you have made any settings changes:

SELECT **S**(ave) to save all of these so that you can use them to print graphs in the future.

Now to print your hard copy:

6   SELECT **Image-Select**. *PrintGraph* lists all the .PIC files.

7   HIGHLIGHT **PIEPRINT** for printing and PRESS SPACE BAR. A # sign will appear in front of the filename. This means it has been selected for printing.

8   PRESS ENTER.

9   Adjust the paper and SELECT **A**(lign).

10   SELECT **G**(o) to begin printing. When finished SELECT **P**(age) to advance the paper. You should now have a print out of a pie chart.

These are the basics for printing graphs. There are many other refinements both within the *PrintGraph* program and the *Wysiwyg* publishing add-in which allow you to change scaling, the way numbers are shown, fonts, rotation etc. Task 34 will introduce you to some of these features.

Activity 17.2 Printing the two graphs PIEPRINT and PRICESP on one page

1   SELECT **S**(ettings) **I**(mage) **S**(ize) **H**(alf) **Q**(uit) *three* times until you get back to the *PrintGraph* main menu.

2   SELECT **I**(mage-Select) and mark the two graphs for printing as above.

3   PRESS ENTER.

4   SELECT **A**(lign) **G**(o).

5   SELECT **P**(age) after printing.

6   SELECT **E**(xit) to leave *Printgraph*.

Key words	**PrintGraph**	**Hardware**
	Settings	**Graph-Directory**
	Image	**Fonts-Directory**
	Size	

Section E: Useful functions

Task 18　**Logical functions**

Objectives　To examine the use of the **@IF** function with simple and complex logical operators.

Instructions　The **@IF** function gives one result if a test (condition) is *true* and a different result if the test is *false*. The syntax is:

@IF(test, action if true, action if false)

@IF can be used with any of the following logical simple operators:

=　equal to
<>　not equal to
<　less than
>　greater than
<=　less than or equal to
>=　greater than or equal to

Activity 18.1 The @IF function

1　TYPE an age less than 17 years into A1 e.g. **15**.

2　In A2 TYPE **@IF(A1>=17,"OK to drive","Too young")**

This means:

Test:　If the figure in A1 is greater than or equal to 17
　　　　then
　　　　　　(TRUE) display "OK to drive"
　　　　else
　　　　　　(FALSE) display "Too young"

3　Now change A1 to any age 17 or over. The test is now true and therefore **"OK to drive"** will appear in A2.

Activity 18.2 Complex logical operators #AND#, #OR# and #NOT#

These can be used together with the **@IF** function. The syntax is:

@IF(Test1#AND#Test2, action if true, action if false)
@IF(Test1#OR#Test2, action if true, action if false)
@IF(Test1#NOT#Test2, action if true, action if false)

1   In A3 TYPE **@IF(A1>5#AND#A1<10,A1*3,0)**

i.e. *both* tests must be *true* to return A1*3

2   In A4 TYPE **@IF(A1=5#OR# B1=7,5,0)**

i.e. *either* of the tests must be *true* to return 5.

3   In A5 TYPE **@IF(#NOT#A1=7,A1+7,0)**

i.e. the *true* result (A1+7) is returned if A1 does #NOT# contain 7.

4   Experiment by changing the figures in A1 and B1 and looking at the results of these tests.

Key words   #AND#
                #OR#
                #NOT#
                @IF

Task 19   Making a date

Objectives   To examine 1-2-3 date functions.
To use these functions in formulae.
To display date in different formats.

Instructions   One of the most useful features of 1-2-3 is its ability to perform arithmetically with dates and to vary their presentation. Each date has a value calculated since January 1st 1900 which is 1. The upper limit is December 31st 2099, 73050 days from the start!

Date functions

@DATE(year,month,day)	gives the number of days between January 1st 1900 and the date provided.
@TODAY	does the same but picks up the system date (today's date if set up correctly).
@DAY(number)	gives the day number in the date.
@MONTH(number)	gives the month number.
@YEAR(number)	gives the year number.

Presentation of dates

The **/ R**(ange) **F**(ormat) **D**(ate) option allows you to choose from three ways of converting the strange date numbers above into understandable forms. You can show dates as:

Day-month-year
Day-month
Month-year

Thus 33089 days since Jan 1st 1900 can be output as 04-Aug-90 *or* 04-Aug *or* as Aug-90 (useful for table headings). Try it with **/RFD1** (and then 2 and 3).

In general use functions like **@DATE** to enter dates into the worksheet and the format options to control their appearance on screen. Remember, if you get asterisks then widen the column with **/WCS10**⃞ENTER⃞, so that the date can be seen.

Activity 19.1 Adding and subtracting dates

Because 1-2-3 stores data in integer form it is easy to determine the number of days between given dates which can be useful in many applications e.g. age debtor analysis, time discounts, determining when to trigger reminder letters etc. NWB shares in Task 20 is one such application.

1   CLEAR the worksheet screen with **/WEY**(es).

2   In A1 TYPE **@TODAY**.

3   In A2 **TYPE @DATE(99,12,25)**.

4   In A3 **TYPE +A2-A1**.

The result is the number of days between now and Christmas 1999.

5   A value can be added to or subtracted from a date to produce a new date e.g. in A1 TYPE **@TODAY+30**. This will return a number for thirty days hence. SELECT **/RFD1** to format this date thirty days from now.

Try the following:

6   CREATE a weekly calendar. (*Hint*: ENTER start date in cell A1 and USE formula A1+7 and COPY down.)

How many days are there between your birthday and Xmas?

7   In A5 TYPE **@DATE(93,12,25)-@DATE(93,10,20)** (use your birthday here).

This will show that there are 66 days between October 20th (the assumed birthday) and Xmas.

Mouse users: CLICK date icon to enter system date into current cell.

Key words **@IF**
              @DATE
              @TODAY
              @DAY
              @MONTH
              @YEAR

Task 20 **A worked example using the @DATE function**

Objective To show more about writing formulae, including dates, and to revise such functions as moving ranges and inserting columns and rows.

Instructions **The Northwest Savings Bank**

This Task involves the buying and selling of shares. The spreadsheet below outlines what you are aiming to achieve. *Note:* There are four parts to the spreadsheet and you will set it up in a slightly different way across the screen so that you can MOVE things around for practise. The full, corrected results appear in the spreadsheet on page 68.

	A	B	C	D	E	F	G
1	Northwest Savings Bank <part1>						
2							
3	Purchase:						
4	==						
5	Date	Shares	Price	Comm(3%)	Cost		
6	————————————————————————————————————						
7	20-Oct-84	100	£0.50	£1.50	£51.50		
8							
9	Sale:	<	part 2	>		<	part 3 >
10	===						
11	Date	Shares	Price	Comm(3%)	Income	Gain(loss)	Term
12	——						
13	28-Dec-86	100	£0.84	£2.52	£81.48	£29.98	Long

Activity 20.1 Buying shares

See part 1 of the spreadsheet.

1 Start with a blank worksheet and ENTER a company title. (For the purposes of this Task **Northwest Savings Bank** has been used but you can use any company name you wish). Next ENTER identification labels. Use arrow keys to speed things up.

2 **In cell:** **ENTER:**
  A3 **Purchase:**
  A5 **Date**
  B5 **Shares**
  C **Price**
  D5 **Comm(3%)**
  E5 **Cost**

3 CENTRE the range of column labels, A5 to E5 by moving to A5 and SELECTING **/ R**(ange) **L**(abel) **C**(entre).

63

Note: As an alternative to the **/ R**(ange) commands given throughout this Section you may prefer to pre-select using F4 or DRAG with the mouse. You can then select the range command **/R** etc *or* CLICK the appropriate icon for the function needed.

4   HIGHLIGHT the range **A5..E5** and PRESS ENTER.

5   Next CREATE the double line that separates the column labels from the section heading.

6   MOVE to A4 and TYPE **\=** (the '\' is the repeat key). PRESS ENTER.

7   Then COPY to **B4..E4**. Use the same procedure to COPY the single line which separates the column labels from the numbers in row 6 (*see* part 1 again).

Activity 20.2 The @DATE function and date format

Usually the date will be a label but if you want to perform calculations on it, for example, the number of days between a purchase and a sale, you use the **@DATE** function.

1   ENTER the share purchase date, **20 October 1984**.

2   MOVE to cell A7.

3   TYPE **@DATE(84,10,20)** - i.e. year, month, day.

A number 30975 appears. This is the number of days between January 1 1900 and October 20 1984. **@DATE** can convert dates between the years 1900 and 2099.

Once **@DATE** has converted the date to a number it can be displayed in a number of formats. To see the options available:

4   SELECT **/ R**(ange) **F**(ormat) **D**(ate).

5   Use the pointer key to read the descriptions. ACCEPT option 1, the standard long form, and at the prompt, HIGHLIGHT all the cells in which you want dates to appear (A7..A9 will do for now). Asterisks will appear in A7 indicating that the date will not fit. WIDEN the column until 20-Oct-84 appears.

6   MOVE to B7 and TYPE **100** ENTER - the number of shares purchased.

7   In C7 TYPE **0.50** ENTER. The share price is 50 pence.

8   In D7 TYPE **+B7*C7*3%** ENTER. Cell D7 should display 1.5.

Change the format to currency:

9   SELECT **/ R**(ange) **F**(ormat) **C**(urrency) ENTER.

10 FORMAT the range C7..E9.

11 Unanchor the pointer with the ESC key.

12 MOVE to C7. Anchor the pointer with the **.** (full stop) and arrow to highlight the

range, then PRESS ENTER.

13 MOVE to E7 and TYPE **+B7*C7+D7** ENTER.

What does this represent? It is the cost of buying shares, i.e. price multiplied by number purchased plus commission.

14 Now SAVE the file, calling it **NWB1**.

15 SELECT **/ F**(ile) **S**(ave) and TYPE **NWB1** PRESS ENTER.

Activity 20.3 Selling shares

See part 2 of the spreadsheet.

1 USE file NWB1. (If it's not on screen SELECT **/ F**(ile) **R**(etrieve) and TYPE *or* HIGHLIGHT the file name).

2 Now COPY the column labels and lines (A4..E6) to F4. Position this section below the existing one later on.

3 MOVE to A4.

4 SELECT **/C**(opy).

5 PRESS RIGHT ARROW four times and DOWN ARROW twice to highlight the range, then PRESS ENTER.

6 MOVE to F4 and PRESS ENTER. 1-2-3 will COPY the labels and lines into a new block starting at cell F4.

Mouse users: DRAG A4..E6, CLICK Copy icon, CLICK F4 twice.

Note: the active area of your spreadsheet is now larger than the display screen and you must point to see some of your copied labels. This is a useful time to practise moving around the screen (*see* Task 1).

7 MOVE to A4.

8 PRESS END key then RIGHT ARROW. This moves the pointer to J4.

9 MOVE to A1 and PRESS END RIGHT ARROW again.

10 This moves thew pointer to IV1 at the far end of the spreadsheet. 1-2-3 will MOVE in the END ARROW direction until the cell contents change from blank to filled or vice-versa.

11 Next TYPE the heading '**Sale:**' in F3. Use the F5 Goto key to get there.

12 MOVE to J5 and CHANGE the label from **Cost** to **Income**. Now ENTER the share sales data. Remember to use the ^ label prefix to centre.

13 In F7 ENTER **@DATE(86,12,28)**. The number 31774 should appear. To display

numbers as dates in column F format cells F7..F9. 28-Dec-86 will appear in F7 (the asterisks indicate that you need to widen a column to display data).

14 TYPE **100** into G7 (i.e. the number of shares sold).

15 ENTER the price per share in H7 (0.84).

16 The broker's commission on the share sale is the same formula as used in D7 so COPY it into the cell. 2.52 should appear in I7.

17 Finally INSERT a formula in J7 to calculate the amount received from the share sale. 81.48 should appear in the cell. (The correct formula is: **+G7*H7-I7** i.e. selling price multiplied by the number of shares minus the commission.)

18 CHANGE the display format of the commission and cost figures to currency.

Activity 20.4 Moving a range

However much planning you do there is often a need to redesign a worksheet. There are many ways of doing this. You can use the **/M**(ove) command to bring our sales section below the purchase part so that you can see everything on the display screen. Alternatively, you can name a range and move it but for the purpose of this Task, highlight it this time.

1 Go to F3.

2 SELECT **/M**(ove) and HIGHLIGHT **F3..J7** at the prompt. PRESS ENTER.

3 MOVE the section to the area which begins in A9 by moving to cell A9 and PRESSING ENTER.

Note: you only need to tell 1-2-3 where to start the 'TO' range.

4 PRESS HOME to view all your work, then SAVE it as **NWB2**.

Mouse users: DRAG F3..J7, CLICK Move icon, CLICK A9 (top left target address). CLICK to confirm.

Activity 20.5 Profits (or losses) on share sales

Set up a section to calculate the profit or loss from each completed transaction and determine whether the gain is long or short term. *See part 3 of the spreadsheet.*

1 **In cell:**   **ENTER:**
    F11   **^Gain (Loss)**
    G11   **^Term**

2 EXTEND the double and single lines in rows 10 and 12 into columns F and G using

the COPY command.

Column F will display gains and losses in amounts up to 5 figures.

3   SET to currency format and WIDEN the column if necessary.

4   In F13 TYPE **+E13-E7** (i.e. sale - purchase cost).

Activity 20.6 The @IF function

You can compare the dates using 1-2-3's **@IF** function.

1   In G13 TYPE **@IF(A13-A7>365," Long"," Short")**.

This means that if the difference between the dates in cells A13 and A7 is greater than 365 days *then* print "Long" *else* print "Short". This is the first time that you have used the @IF function in a serious application. You can see that it can be a very useful tool in spreadsheet work.

In general the syntax for the IF test is:

@IF(comparison,result-if-true,result-if-false).

"Long" should appear as a result of the formula.

2   SAVE your worksheet as **NWB3**.

Activity 20.7 Entering additional data

See part 4 (on page 68) of the spreadsheet.

Blank rows or columns can be created to tidy up presentation or to fit extra data. Now enter data for two more share purchases and sales.

1   MOVE to A8.

2   SELECT **/Worksheet Insert Row**.

3   HIGHLIGHT **A8..A9** and PRESS ENTER.

This will create two blank rows for the new data. (Use **/ W**(orksheet) **D**(elete) to get rid of columns or rows.)

4   ENTER the dates, number of shares purchased and prices only for the Robber Baron and K9P shares (as shown in the spreadsheet on page 68) into cells B8 to C9.

5   ENTER the share names into F7..F9 and the heading into F5.

6   COPY them to H13..H17 as appropriate.

7   MOVE to D7 and SELECT **/ C**(opy).
     What? D7..E7 **To Where?** D8..E9.

8   FORMAT cells as appropriate.

9   ENTER data in cells A16 to C17 (i.e. dates, number of shares sold and prices only).

10   Again COPY the formulae in E15..G15 into E16..G17

     Range to copy what?: E15..G15
     Range to copy to where?: E16..G17.

11   SAVE your worksheet as **NWB4** and PRINT it out. *Note:* you can delete earlier
     NWB files now if you wish.

Activity 20.8

Can you see the fatal flaw in the model? You are apparently losing £396.63 on your
ROBBER BARON shares. The model assumed that you always sell all the shares in one
go and yet you have only sold half of those shares. Amend the formula to correct the
model.

1   In F15 TYPE **+E15-(B15*C7*1.03)** and COPY down the column to F16..F17.

In other words, sales income (in E15) minus the cost of purchasing the same number of
shares (number in B15 multiplied by the cost in C7 plus 3%).

	A	B	C	D	E	F	G	H
1	Northwest Savings Bank <part4>							
2								
3	Purchase:							
4	==							
5	Date	Shares	Price	Comm(3%)	Cost	Share name		
6	———							
7	20-Oct-84	100	£0.50	£1.50	£51.50	GT Industries		
8	25-Dec-85	500	£1.50	£22.50	£772.50	Robber Baron		
9	07-Apr-91	200	£1.00	£6.00	£206.00	K9P		
10								
11	Sale:							
12	==							
13	Date	Shares	Price	Comm(3%)	Income	Gain(loss)	Term	Share name
14	———							
15	28-Dec-86	100	£0.84	£2.52	£81.48	£29.98	Long	GT Industries
16	30-Nov-86	250	£1.55	£11.63	£375.88	(£10.38)	Short	Robber Baron
17	01-Oct-91	200	£1.12	£6.72	£217.28	£11.28	Short	K9P

To print your worksheet, *either* SELECT narrow columns with **/WCS** *and/or*
SELECT condensed print (setup string \015 in 1-2-3).

Key words @DATE
@IF

Task 21   1-2-3's 'word processor' and text handling

Objective   To use 1-2-3 string functions.

Instructions   1-2-3 has very basic text handling facilities. These are useful for writing short paragraphs etc about the spreadsheet figures or graphs.

As`well as words and symbols, 1-2-3 will also treat as text labels any numbers or mathematical symbols which are given a label prefix ('^'). ^12345 would therefore be treated as text.

Activity 21.1 String functions

"*String*" is the computing term for letters and symbols which are "strung" together. These functions help you to manipulate text. You can use a string function to change to upper or lower case, locate portions of text, replace text or show special characters.

Try out the functions below; instructions are in the left-hand column, results in the right. Explanations of each function appear afterwards.

```
A:F14: @TRIM("     Mr  Soft  ")                                           READY
```

	A	B	C	D	E	F	G	H
1	In cell F1 type string functions <Enter>					string functions		
2	In F2 type @UPPER(F1)					STRING FUNCTIONS		
3	In F3 type @LOWER(F2)					string functions		
4	In F4 type @LEFT(F1,6)					string		
5	In F5 type @RIGHT(F1,9)					functions		
6	In F6 type @MID(F1,2,4)					ring		
7	In F7 type @LENGTH(F1)					16		
8	In F8 type @REPEAT(F6,3)					ringringring		
9	In F9 type @FIND("f",F1,0)					7		
10	In F10 type change!					change!		
11	In F11 type @REPLACE(F1,7,9,F10)					string change!		
12	In F12 type @CHAR(65)					A		
13	In F13 type @PROPER(F5)					Functions		
14	In F14 type @TRIM(" Mr Soft ")							
15	In F15 type:					You've won 16 coupons!		
16	+"You've won "&@STRING(F7,0)&" coupons!"							
17	In F17 type @EXACT(F4,f6)					0		
18	In F18 type @ISSTRING(F7)					0		
19								
20								

STRING.WK1

Explanations

1 Enters sample text - string functions
2 Changes it to upper case
3 Changes it to lower case
4 Displays leftmost 6 characters, i.e. string
5 Displays rightmost 9 characters, i.e. functions
6 Displays 4 characters starting at the 2nd one, i.e. ring
7 Displays the number of characters in the string - 16
8 Repeats ring 3 times
9 Finds little "f" the 7th character in the string
10 Enters sample text string in F10 - *change*
11 Rreplaces *functions* in F1 with F10 string i.e. change
12 Returns ASCII value (in this case capital A although control characters can also be produced
13 Converts string in F5 so that the first letter is a capital
14 Removes leading, trailing and extra embedded spaces from the string *Mr Soft*
15 Converts a number (in F7, 0 decimal places) to a label - the &'s link the text
16 Determines if 2 character strings are identical - 1 = true, 0 = false
17 Finds if cell entry is a label - 1 = true, 0 = false

Key word   String

Section F: Lookup tables and linking files ■■■

Task 22   ## Lookup tables

Objective   To set up a lookup table for referencing.

Instructions   1-2-3 has a Lookup function which allows you to search a table for an appropriate value to use in your worksheet. There are two lookup functions in 1-2-3 - a **V**(ertical) one for columns and a **H**(orizontal) one for rows. As they operate in exactly the same way this Task will examine just the first one.

In 1-2-3 the **@VLOOKUP** function can be used to "look up" a value or code in a table. The first column of the table contains sequential values or letters and the adjacent columns the values or text which are being looked up. The lookup table is set up in a clear area of the spreadsheet but can be viewed on screen with the data if the screen is split into two windows.

The format for the **@VLOOKUP** function is:

@VLOOKUP(Value, Lookup table range, column offset).

Value
This is the value or cell reference holding the value to be looked up. If the value does not match the spreadsheet value then 1-2-3 takes the nearest value rounded down. If the value is smaller than anything in LOOKUP, 1-2-3 returns ERR; anything larger will give the highest value.

Lookup table range
This is the range of cells containing the lookup table.

Column offset
This is the number of columns from the first column (unfortunately counted as column 0) in the lookup range.

The lookup function is very useful for such applications as tax tables, price lists, exchange rates etc. For example, look at a customer invoice.

Activity 22.1 Creating and naming lookup tables

You are now going to create two lookup tables to find customer names and then discount amounts.

1   TYPE in the following. Again make sure that you use the same cell locations.

	A	B	C	D	E	F
1	PRODUCT: GO-FASTER RUNNING SHOES					
2	PRICE	29.99				
3						
4	Customer	Customer	Order	Order	Discount	Invoice
5	code	name	Quantity	Value		Total
6	140		70			
7	150		210			
8	120		35			
9	180		125			
10	160		10			
11	170		175			
12	130		50			
13						
14	LOOKUP TABLES for:					
15	Customer name			Quantity	Discount rate	
16	120	Alf Tupper		0	0.00%	
17	130	Lee Evans		50	5.00%	
18	140	Carl Lewis		100	10.00%	
19	150	Steve Jones		150	15.00%	
20	160	Gordon Jibson		200	20.00%	
21	170	Fred Carno				
22	180	Carlos Lopez				

2 Widen column B to accept names longer than 9 characters.

3 MOVE to column B.

4 SELECT **/WCS 14**.

Note: cells E16 to E20 are in percent format.

5 SELECT **/RFP 2** and highlight this range of cells.

For easier referencing it is advisable to name the lookup tables.

6 MOVE to A16.

7 SELECT **/RNC** and call it **CUSTNAME**.

8 HIGHLIGHT range A16..B22 ENTER.

9 MOVE to D16.

10 SELECT **/RNC** and call it **DISCOUNT**.

11 HIGHLIGHT the range D16..E20 ENTER.

Activity 22.2 Using the formulae

1 In B6 TYPE **@VLOOKUP(A6,$CUSTNAME,1)**.

This means the value in A6 (code 140) will be looked up in the CUSTNAME lookup table, column 0. The resulting name found in column 1 will be returned in B6.

2 Now COPY the formula down to B12.

3 SELECT **/C**(opy) **B6** to **B7..B12**.

Note: this is another example of *mixed* copying i.e. the cell reference for value will change *relative* to the spreadsheet position from A6 to A7 etc, but the reference to the lookup table CUSTNAME will be fixed so the $ sign will be added. This is 1-2-3's way of copying *absolutely*.

4 MOVE to D6 and TYPE **+$B$2*C6** i.e. the price (£29.99 in B2) multiplied by the order quantity.

5 COPY the formula down to D12 as above.

6 MOVE to E6 and TYPE **@VLOOKUP(C6,$DISCOUNT,1)*D6** i.e. check the order quantity in C6 against the lookup table DISCOUNT and return the discount rate.

7 COPY the formula down to E12 as above.

8 MOVE to F6 and TYPE **+D6-E6** i.e. the invoice total (the amount to bill the customer) is order value minus discount received.

9 COPY the formula down to F12. CHECK all your work with the completed results and formulae below.

	A	B	C	D	E	F
1	PRODUCT: GO FASTER RUNNING SHOES					
2	PRICE	29.99				
3						
4	Customer	Customer	Order	Order	Discount	Invoice
5	code	name	Quantity	Value		Total
6	140	Carl Lewis	70	2099.30	104.97	1994.34
7	150	Steve Jones	210	6297.90	1259.58	5038.32
8	120	Alf Tupper	35	1049.65	0.00	1049.65
9	180	Carlos Lopez	125	3748.75	347.88	3373.88
10	160	Gordon Jibson	10	299.90	0.00	299.90
11	170	Fred Carno	175	5248.25	787.24	4461.01
12	130	Lee Evans	50	1499.50	74.98	1424.53

FORMULAS USED:

Customer code	Customer name
140	@IF(@VLOOKUP(A6,$CUSTNAME,0)=A6,@VLOOKUP(A6,$CUSTNAME,1)"Wrong code")
150	@IF(@VLOOKUP(A7,$CUSTNAME,0)=A7,@VLOOKUP(A6,$CUSTNAME,1)"Wrong code")
120	@IF(@VLOOKUP(A8,$CUSTNAME,0)=A8,@VLOOKUP(A6,$CUSTNAME,1)"Wrong code")
180	@IF(@VLOOKUP(A9,$CUSTNAME,0)=A9,@VLOOKUP(A6,$CUSTNAME,1)"Wrong code")
160	@IF(@VLOOKUP(A10,$CUSTNAME,0)=A10,@VLOOKUP(A6,$CUSTNAME,1)"Wrong code")
170	@IF(@VLOOKUP(A11,$CUSTNAME,0)=A11,@VLOOKUP(A6,$CUSTNAME,1)"Wrong code")
130	@IF(@VLOOKUP(A12,$CUSTNAME,0)=A12,@VLOOKUP(A6,$CUSTNAME,1)"Wrong code")

Order quantity	Order value	Discount	Invoice total
70	+$B$2*C6	@VLOOKUP(C6,$DISCOUNT,1)*D6	+D6-E6
210	+$B$2*C7	@VLOOKUP(C7,$DISCOUNT,1)*D6	+D7-E7
35	+$B$2*C8	@VLOOKUP(C8,$DISCOUNT,1)*D6	+D8-E8
125	+$B$2*C9	@VLOOKUP(C9,$DISCOUNT,1)*D6	+D9-E9
10	+$B$2*C10	@VLOOKUP(C10,$DISCOUNT,1)*D6	+D10-E10
175	+$B$2*C11	@VLOOKUP(C11,$DISCOUNT,1)*D6	+D11-E11
50	+$B$2*C12	@VLOOKUP(C12,$DISCOUNT,1)*D6	+D12-E12

Activity 22.3 To split the screen into two windows

1 GOTO row 14.

2 SELECT **/ W**(orksheet) **W**(indow) **H**(orizontal) to split the screen horizontally.

3 PRESS F6 to move between the two windows.

4 SELECT **/WWC**(lear) to clear windows and return to the full screen display.

Activity 22.4 Lookups which require an exact match

If the value or code has to be an exact match, what happens if the wrong code is entered? For example, in the spreadsheet on page 00 try the following codes in cell A6: 110, 200, 156. They return ERR (lower than the first code), Carlos Lopez (highest available code) and Steve Jones (nearest code rounded down) respectively.

Clearly it's desirable to have an exact match so:

1 TYPE the following formula in B6:

@IF(@VLOOKUP(A6,$CUSTNAME,0)=A6,@VLOOKUP(A6,$CUSTNAME,1),"Wrong code").

See Task 18 for more information on @IF

2   COPY it down to B12.

Now any customer code above 120 (the lower limit) that doesn't have an exact match in the CUSTNAME lookup table will return "**Wrong code**". It can then be re-entered correctly. To eliminate the ERR(or) message for codes less than 120 do the following:

3   MOVE to row 16.

4   SELECT **/ W**(orksheet) **I**(nsert) **R**(ow) ENTER.

5   In A16 TYPE **0**.

6   In B16 TYPE **Wrong code**.

7   SELECT **/ R**(ange) **N**(ame) **C**(reate).

8   HIGHLIGHT CUSTNAME and amend the range, TYPE **A16..B23** ENTER.

Incorrect codes from 0 to 119 will now show Wrong code rather than ERR. To **save** the spreadsheet:

9   SELECT **/FS** and call it **LOOKUP**.

Key words **@VLOOKUP**   **Lookup table range**
                Value   **Column offset**
                Window

Task 23   **Linking files**

Objectives   To name ranges to make links.
To create links between files.
To list named ranges in a worksheet.
To list target and linked source files.

Instructions   File linking lets you use, in your current worksheet, the values from other worksheet files
which are saved on disk. In this exercise you will look at a shop group. Although the
group has many shops nationwide, for the purpose of this task you will deal with just two.
You will then use data from these *source* files in a *target* file called LINK which will extract
data from both. File linking saves manual updating because any change to the source
files will be reflected automatically in the target file.

You are going to:

* Retrieve worksheet SGR2 (from page 31, Task 9) add a label and save it as
  SLOUGH, for the Slough shop.
* Change some figures and save it as HULL, for the Hull shop.
* Create a target file called LINK.

Activity 23.1 Creating source files

1   SELECT **/ F**(ile) **R**(etrieve)**SGR2** (*see* screen display below).

A:A11: [W13] 'Net Profit   `READY`

A	B	C	D	E	F	G
1		SUE,GRABBIT and RUN				
2		SLOUGH STORE				
3						
4		Jan	Feb	March	April	YTD
5	Sales income	100000	120000	150000	170000	540000
6	Cost of sales	60000	70000	90000	100000	320000
7		----------	----------	----------	----------	----------
8	Gross Profit	40000	50000	60000	70000	220000
9	Overheads	15000	18000	22500	25500	81000
10		----------	----------	----------	----------	----------
11	Net Profit	25000	32000	37500	44500	139000
12		==========	==========	==========	==========	==========
13						
14	source filename SLOUGH					
15						
16						
17						
18						
19						
20						

SLOUGH.WK1

Imagine that this is the Profit Statement for one shop in a nationwide store chain.

2 TYPE the label **SLOUGH STORE** in cell C2.

Name the following ranges in this source file.

3 MOVE the cell pointer to F5.

4 SELECT **/RNC**.

5 TYPE **YTD-SALES** ENTER and ENTER again to accept range F5.

6 MOVE to F6.

7 SELECT **/RNC** (as 2 above).

8 TYPE **YTD-COST** ENTER ENTER.

9 MOVE to cell F11.

10 SELECT **/RNC** (as 2 above).

11 TYPE **YTD-PROFIT** ENTER ENTER.

These cells can now be referenced by name in the target file.

12 SELECT **/ F**(ile) **S**(ave) and SAVE it as **SLOUGH**.

To save time creating another source file, edit this one for another shop in the chain.

13 TYPE **HULL STORE** in cell C2.

14 CHANGE the following eight **sales** and **cost of sales** figures as follows:

columns	B	C	D	E
rows 5	50000	20000	25000	33500
6	22750	35000	12340	15000

15 CREATE the range names in this file as for the Slough file:

YTD-SALES in F5, **YTD-COST** in F6 and **YTD-PROFIT** in F11.

16 SELECT **/ F**(ile) **S**(ave) and SAVE the HULL STORE file as **HULL**.

```
   A          A              B        C        D        E        F        G
 1                          SUE,GRABBIT and RUN
 2                          HULL STORE
 3
 4                      Jan      Feb    March    April      YTD
 5  Sales income       50000    20000    25000    33500   128500
 6  Cost of sales      22750    35000    12340    15000    85090
 7                   -------------------------------------------------
 8  Gross Profit       27250   -15000    12660    18500    43410
 9  Overheads           7500     3000     3750     5025    19275
10                   -------------------------------------------------
11  Net Profit         19750   -18000     8910    13475    24135
12                   =================================================
13
14  source filename HULL
15
16
17
18
19
20
```
HULL.WK1

Activity 23.2 Creating the target (linked) file

Set up the target file LINK.

1 SELECT **/WE**(rase) **Y**(es) to erase the current worksheet and create the following.

2 TYPE in the labels in the appropriate cells following the layout below.

	A	B	C	D	E	F	G	H
1		SUE,GRABBIT and RUN						
2		COMPANY PROFIT STATEMENT 19-2						
3								
4								
5						DIFFERENCE		
6	YTD	COST OF	NET	% PROFIT		PLANNED	ACTUAL - PLANNED	
7		SALES	PROFIT	ON SALES		PROFITS	PROFIT	
8								
9	SLOUGH							
10	HULL							
11	---------	-----------	---------	-----------	---	----------	-----------	---------
12	TOTAL							
13								
14	target filename LINK							

If you enter the right formulae, 1-2-3 will pull in figures for **sales**, **cost of sales** and **actual net profits** from the SLOUGH and HULL source files. You can then create further formulae for the rest. The general format for linking formula is:

+<<source file name>>source range name

3 SELECT **/ W**(orksheet) **G**(lobal) **D**(efault) **O**(ther) **C**(lock) **F**(ilename). This is useful when you are working with files as it shows file names on the status line at the bottom of the screen.

4 MOVE to B9.

5 TYPE **+<<SLOUGH>>$YTD-SALES**.

6 MOVE to C9.

7 TYPE **+<<SLOUGH>>$YTD-COST**.

Note: it may be quicker to COPY the formula in B9 across and edit it.

8 MOVE to D9.

9 TYPE **+<<SLOUGH>>$YTD-PROFIT**.

You will see that the figures from the SLOUGH file have appeared.

10 In cells B10, C10 and D10, repeat the procedure above for the HULL file substituting HULL for SLOUGH i.e. in B10 TYPE **+<<HULL>>$YTD-SALES** etc.

11 Now MOVE to E9.

12 TYPE **+D9/B9**. This will divide actual profits by sales.

13 SELECT **/ R**(ange) **F**(ormat) **P**(ercent) **0** to change the format to %.

14 MOVE to F9.

15 TYPE **125000**.

16 MOVE to F10.

17 TYPE **32000**.

These are head office estimates for the branch profits.

18 MOVE to G9.

19 TYPE **+D9-F9**. This is the difference between actual and planned profits.

20 MOVE to H9.

21 TYPE **@IF(@ABS(+G9/F9)>15%,"ACTION"," ")**.

This long formula means 'If the planned and actual profits differ by more than 15% either way (+ or -) then ACTION should be printed to warn management, otherwise leave blank'. **@ABS** returns the ABSolute figure without the + or - sign.

This is a good example of *exception reporting*. Head Office is apparently concerned with variances + or - 15% in this case.

22 SELECT **/C**(opy) and COPY the formula **FROM E9..H9 TO E10..H10**.

23 MOVE to B12.

24 TYPE **@SUM(B9..B10)**. This will total the shop sales.

25 SELECT **/ C**(opy) **FROM B12 TO C12..G12**. This will add the other figures.

To improve the appearance of cell E12 calculate a crude average:

26 In E12 TYPE **@AVG(E9..E10)**. (@AVG will give the average {arithmetic mean} for this range of data).

27 SELECT **/ R**(ange) **F**(ormat) **P**(ercent) **0** to convert to a percentage figure.

28 CHECK your final results with the following.

	A	B	C	D	E	F	G	H
1		SUE,GRABBIT and RUN						
2		COMPANY PROFIT STATEMENT 19-2						
3								
4								
5						DIFFERENCE		
6		YTD	COST OF	NET	% PROFIT	PLANNED	ACTUAL -	PLANNED
7		SALES	SALES	PROFIT	ON SALES	PROFITS	PROFIT	
8								
9	SLOUGH	540000	320000	139000	26%	125000	14000	
10	HULL	128500	85090	24135	19%	32000	-7865	ACTION
11		--						
12	TOTAL	668500	85090	163135	22%	157000	6135	
13								
14	target filename LINK							

If you wish to, print the file:

29 SELECT **/PPR(A1.. H12)G**.

30 SELECT **/FS** and call the file **LINK**.

For your reference every cell entry is shown below.

31 To print underlying formulae: SELECT **/ P**(rint) **P**(rinter) **R**(ange) **O**(ptions) **O**(ther) **C**(ell-Formulas).

```
B2  :  'SUE,GRABBIT AND RUN
B3  :  'COMPANY PROFIT STATEMENT 19-2
D5  :  "ACTUAL
G5  :  "DIFFERENCE
B6  :  ^YTD
C6  :  "COST OF
D6  :  '  NET
E6  :  "% PROFIT
F6  :  "PLANNED
G6  :  "ACTUAL - PLANNED
B7  :  "SALES
C7  :  ' SALES
D7  :  "PROFIT
E7  :  "ON SALES
F7  :  "PROFITS
G7  :  'PROFIT
A9  :  'SLOUGH
B9  :  +<<SLOUGH.WK1>>$YTD-SALES
C9  :  +<<SLOUGH.WK1>>$YTD-COST
D9  :  +<<SLOUGH.WK1>>$YTD-PROFIT
E9  :  (PO) +D9/B9
F9  :  125000
G9  :  +D9-F9
A10 :  'HULL
B10 :  +<<HULL.WK1>>$YTD-SALES
C10 :  +<<HULL.WK1>>$YTD-SALES
D10 :  +<<HULL.WK1>>$YTD-SALES
E10 :  (PO) +D10/B10
F10 :  32000
G10 :  +D10-F10
A11 :  \-
B11 :  \-
C11 :  \-
D11 :  \-
E11 :  \-
F11 :  \-
G11 :  \-
A12 :  'TOTAL
B12 :  @SUM(B9..B10)
C12 :  @SUM(C9..C10)
D12 :  @SUM(D9..D10)
E12 :  (PO) @AVG(E9..E10)
F12 :  @SUM(F9..F10)
G12 :  @SUM(G9..G10)
A14 :  'target filename LINK
```

Activity 23.3 The acid test

1 To retrieve the SLOUGH file: SELECT **/FR SLOUGH**.

2 CHANGE the January sales figure to 40000 and SAVE the file.

3 Now call up the LINK file. You will see that the figures from SLOUGH have been automatically updated.

4 To display a list of linked files: SELECT **/ F**(ile) **L**(ist) **L**(inked).

5 USE the ARROW keys to see the information for each linked file. PRESS ENTER to return to *ready* mode.

Key words Source file
Target file
@ABS
@AVG

Section G: Database management ▪▪▪▪

Task 24
Using a 1-2-3 database

Objective   To set up and sort a database in 1-2-3.

Instructions   1-2-3 allows you to set up and use simple databases arranged by rows and columns. A database is a collection of **records** about a person or item. Within each record there are a number of **fields** containing data. For example, a stock record might contain the following fields: item number, name, quantity in stock, price, reorder quantity etc. 1-2-3 stores each record in a separate row and each field is stored in a separate cell.

Database management is useful because you can perform the following functions easily and quickly:

- **Sort** records
- **Search** and **find** records
- **Extract** specified records
- **Calculate** with numeric fields
- **Report**
- **Delete** records

Activity 24.1 Creating a database

Set up the sample staff database in the format shown below.

	A	B	C	D	E	F	G	H
1	STAFF	DATABASE						
2								
3	EMPNO	FIRSTNAME	SURNAME	SEX	SALARY	DEPARTMENT	DOB	fieldname
4	1	CHRIS	WADDLE	M	1600	ACCOUNTS	20-Oct-53	
5	2	PAUL	GASCOINE	M	18500	PERSONNEL	18-Jul-63	
6	3	ANNE	SUTTLE	F	20000	MARKETING	15-Dec-56	record
7	4	JOHN	FINCH	M	25000	PURCHASING	03-Mar-50	
8	5	DAVE	SHEARGOLD	M	30000	MARKETING	29-Mar-47	
9	6	BOB	LOMAS	M	18250	ACCOUNTS	25-Dec-63	field
10	7	MARGARET	OWEN	F	21750	PERSONNEL	20-Oct-60	
11	8	JUDY	CASSELLS	F	12500	PURCHASING	21-Mar-34	
12	9	ILENE	DOVER	F	14000	ACCOUNTS	20-Oct-53	
13	10	ALAN	WAINWRIGHT	M	9500	ACCOUNTS	07-Feb-68	
14	11	GILLIAN	WHITEHEAD	F	15500	MARKETING	06-Mar-55	
15	12	DOUG	TAYLOR	M	23500	PERSONNEL	16-Aug-53	
16	13	DES	WALKER	M	27500	ACCOUNTS	02-Jan-65	
17	14	DEL	AMITRI	F	19750	MARKETING	18-Nov-63	
18	15	PETER	GABRIEL	M	22000	PERSONNEL	20-Dec-49	

19	16	ANDY	TOPLIS	M	9500	ACCOUNTS	17-NOV-47
20	17	JURGEN	KLINSMAN	M	12500	PERSONNEL	04-Mar-66
21	18	GLADYS	HEYWOOD	F	16000	PURCHASING	10-Oct-53
22	19	GRAHAM	GREEN	M	35000	MARKETING	07-Feb68
23	20	KIM	BASINGER	F	14500	ACCOUNTS	06-Jun-55
24							

- Plan the design. For example, think about what data you need to keep and why, whether you need to code any data and whether the records should be numbered.

1 TYPE the **field names** in the first row, records follow. Field names are the labels at the top of each column in row 3.

- A field name must be a unique label and must be entered in a single cell. Use a name which identifies the data held in the field. Your sample database fieldnames are self-explanatory except for the two abbreviated ones: EMPNO = Employer Number; DOB = Date of Birth.

2 TYPE each record underneath the field names. Start each record in a new row.

- Do not include blank rows or dividing lines in your database, not even between the fieldname row and the first record.

- Data entries in the field must be all text (labels) or all numbers (values) *not* both.

3 SELECT **/ R**(ange) **F**(ormat) commands to produce the right layout and format, e.g. for dates SELECT **/ R**(ange) **F**(ormat) **D**(ate) **1** ENTER TYPE **G4..G23** ENTER.

- **Justify** text as appropriate with **/ R**(ange) **L**(abel).

- **Data Fill** is a quick way of entering a sequence of numbers with the same incremental value in a specified range.

4 MOVE to **A4**.

5 SELECT **/ D**(ata) **F**(ill).

When asked for the fill range:

6 TYPE **.** (full stop) to anchor, and PRESS DOWN ARROW to highlight down to **A23** and then PRESS ENTER.

7 When asked for a start value TYPE **1** ENTER.

8 Now SELECT the step size **1** ENTER and finally the upper limit, which is already big enough, so just PRESS ENTER.

This will fill in the numbers 1 to 20 in column A.

9   Move to **row 4** and SELECT **/** **W**(orksheet) **T**(itles) **H**(orizontal) to freeze the field names on screen, i.e. all rows above the cell pointer. This will help you to put data in the correct column as your database gets larger than the screen size.

10   **S**(ave) the database.

Note: there are 20 **records** each containing 7 fields. Practise moving around the database using the pointer movement keys. This is important as your databases get bigger.

Activity 24.2 Sorting a database

You can see that the records are currently ordered by employee number.
(*Note*: did you use **/** **D**(ata) **F**(ill) to create this column?)

You are now going to sort the records alphabetically by last name. This involves specifying a:

- range to sort
- field(s) to sort by
- sort order - **A**(scending) will give A-Z or 1-9
  D(escending) will reverse the order.

1   SELECT **/** **D**(ata) **S**(ort) and a settings sheet will appear.

2   SELECT **D**(ata-Range) and HIGHLIGHT all the records and fields in the database by pointing to or typing the cell range **A4 to G23**. The settings sheet will display this.

Note: You do *not* wish to sort the field names.

3   SELECT **P**(rimary-Key) and move to any cell in the SURNAME field and PRESS
ENTER.

4   SELECT **A** for Ascending order (A-Z).

5   SELECT **G**(o) to sort the records.

The records will now appear in surname order.

Activity 24.3 Sorting using two keys

Now organise the records to appear in alphabetical order by SURNAME but within DEPARTMENT.

1   SELECT **/** **D**(ata) **S**(ort).

The settings sheet will appear again. As you are using the same data range (A4 to G23):

2   SELECT **P**(rimary-key) and move to any cell in the DEPARTMENT field and PRESS ENTER.

3   SELECT **A** for Ascending order.

4   SELECT **S**(econdary-key) and MOVE to any cell in the SURNAME field and PRESS ENTER.

5   SELECT **A** for Ascending order (A-Z).

6   SELECT **G**(o) to sort the records.

You should now see all the people in ACCOUNTS in alphabetical order by SURNAME and so on.

Activity 24.4 Further practice

1   SORT the database by DOB (Date Of Birth) showing the youngest first.

2   SORT the database with females first in salary order.

3   SORT the database back to its original order (by EMPNO).

4   SELECT **/ F**(ile) **S**(ave) and save the original file calling it **STAFF**.

Answers

	Primary key	*Order*	*Secondary key*	*Order*
1	DOB	D		
2	SEX	A	SALARY	A
3	EMPNO	A		

Key words	**Record**	**Ascending**
	Field	**Descending**
	Secondary key	**Data Range**
	Data Fill	**Primary key**
	Data Sort	

Searching a database

Objectives   To show how to set up search criteria to find specific records.
To extract those records from the database.
To delete records from the database.

Instructions   You can search for particular records in a database that meet selected criteria. This is
invaluable if your database is large. It is useful to freeze titles by SELECTING
/ W(orksheet) **T**(itles) if you have a large number of records and fields.
You are going to find all of the females in our sample file named STAFF. Retrieve this file
if you have to.
Setting up a query is a five-stage process.

Activity 25.1 Searching for data

Set up a criteria range

1   **/ C**(opy) **A3..G3** (the field names) into **A25** (remember 1-2-3 will remember the
range shape). You have copied all of the field names so that other searches can be
easily carried out.

Enter the criteria

2   In the cell beneath SEX (i.e. **D26**). TYPE **F** (you are searching for females).

```
CRITERIA for finding females (SEX = F)
        A       B        C        D    E        F          G

24
25   EMPNO FIRSTNAME SURNAME   SEX SALARY   DEPARTMENT   DOB
26                             F
27
```

Specify the criteria range

3   SELECT **/ D**(ata) **Q**(uery). The Data Query settings sheet appears.

4   SELECT **C**(riteria).

5   HIGHLIGHT or TYPE **A25..G26** i.e. one row of field names and one row of
criteria.

Specify the input range

This is the database that you wish to search and is similar to the data range you
specified for sorting except that you must include the field names as well as the records.

6   SELECT **I**(nput).

7   HIGHLIGHT or TYPE **A3..G23**.

Find records in the database

8   SELECT **F**(ind).

The first female (**Anne Suttle**) should be highlighted.

9   PRESS DOWN ARROW for the next one, and so on until the end of the database. 1-2-3 will give an audible beep after the last record found.

10 PRESS ESC then **Q**(uit).

Now find all the females earning £15000 or more:

11 Go to cell **E26** and TYPE **>=15000**.

Cell E26 is just below the SALARY field name in the criteria range. The formula says: *is the salary figure equal to or greater than £15000?* As you have already set up the input and criteria ranges and the SEX = F criteria you can proceed.

12 SELECT **/ D**(ata) **Q**(uery) **F**(ind). The first female earning £15000 or more (Anne again) is highlighted.

13 PRESS DOWN ARROW to see the other records that pass the tests. Instead of selecting **/DQF** you can repeat the command by using the F7 query function key. PRESS ESC after the last record is found.

Activity 25.2 Editing while searching

You can edit any field of a highlighted record while searching.

1 SELECT **/ D**(ata) **Q**(uery) **F**(ind) or F7.

2 PRESS DOWN ARROW DOWN ARROW to **Gillian Whitehead's** record.

3 PRESS F7 and then PRESS RIGHT ARROW 4 times to the salary field.

4 PRESS F2 (edit) and change her salary to **17500**.

5 PRESS F7 to start the search again.

The following **operators** are valid in database searches:

< = > mean less than, equal to and greater than and can be used in combination e.g. **>= 10000** would find all records greater than or equal to 10000.
Special characters can be used when searching for text:

* ~   excludes characters e.g. **~ACCOUNTS** finds all records *except* those containing ACCOUNTS.
* *   finds any group of characters after it e.g. **C*** will find any label beginning with **C** - CRUD, CRUDE and CRUDITY.

? finds any single character e.g. P??T will find four-letter labels such as PINT, PART and PRAT.

1-2-3 will also let you search using **AND**, **OR** and **NOT** logic.

Place the criteria on the same row if you want an AND test.

e.g. **SEX   DEPARTMENT**
   M   PERSONNEL

This will find all the men in personnel.

Put the criteria on separate rows if you want an OR test.

e.g. **SEX   DEPARTMENT**
   M

   PERSONNEL

This will find all the men *or* anyone working in personnel.

Remember to adjust the criterion range when using more lines.

Activity 25.3 Further practice

1   FIND people earning between £15000 and £20000.

2   FIND people whose surname begins with G.

3   FIND everyone in *either* PERSONNEL or MARKETING.

Answers

1   MOVE to **D26**. PRESS DEL to delete F.
   In cell E26 edit to **+E4>=15000#AND#+E4<=20000** (using logic AND). The formula says: *is the salary figure in E4 (the first entry in the database input range) between £15000 and £20000?*
   Note: in E26 the figure 1 is shown. This denotes that the result of the test is true (0 is false).

2   In **E26** PRESS DEL and TYPE **G*** into **C26**. The * is a wild card which will match all characters to the end of the label.

3   PRESS DEL in **C26** to delete and TYPE **PERSONNEL** in cell **F26** and **MARKETING** in cell **F27**.
   REDIFINE the criteria range to include cell **F27** i.e. SELECT **/ D**(ata) **Q**(uery) **C**(riteria) **A25..G27**, then **F**(ind).
   Note: the separate rows for the OR test.

Extracting records

Sometimes it is useful to show your selected records separately from the database in what is called the *Output area*. These can be examined on screen or printed out. Using the input range, criteria and criteria range from the last example you are going to extract all of the people from the PERSONNEL department.

If you select a single row for the output range i.e. the field names row, 1-2-3 will take up as many rows as needed to show the extracted records. However, it will erase data that gets in the way so it may be prudent to specify several rows. If the range is too small to fit the extract, 1-2-3 will beep at you with an error message. If this happens PRESS ESC and enlarge the output area.

Activity 25.4

1   SELECT / **D**(ata) **Q**(uery) **C**(riteria) and AMEND range to **A25..G26** (cutting off the MARKETING test). *Alternatively* you could MOVE to cell **F27** and PRESS DEL to remove it.

2   / **Copy** the field names (**A3..F3**) to cell **A30**.

Note: You do not have to COPY all of the field names and they can be put in any order in the output range e.g. we have left off DOB.

3   SWAP FIRSTNAME and SURNAME in **B30** and **C30** to prove it.

4   SELECT / **D**(ata) **Q**(uery) **O**(utput). DEFINE range **A30..F30**.

5   SELECT **E**(xtract) **Q**(uit) to return to *ready* mode.

6   MOVE the cell pointer to **A30** to see your results. They should look as follows:

```
EXTRACTED file - people in PERSONNEL
         A          B            C            D      E            F               G
24
25 EMPNO   FIRSTNAME    SURNAME      SEX    SALARY       DEPARTMENT      DOB
26                                                       PERSONNEL
27
28
29
30 EMPNO   SURNAME      FIRSTNAME    SEX    SALARY       DEPARTMENT      DOB
31     2   GASCOINE     PAUL         M      18500        PERSONNEL
32     7   OWEN         MARGARET     F      21750        PERSONNEL
33    12   TAYLOR       DOUG         M      23500        PERSONNEL
34    15   GABRIEL      PETER        M      22000        PERSONNEL
35    17   KLINSMAN     JURGEN       M      12500        PERSONNEL
```

7   SAVE your spreadsheet calling it **STAFF**.

Activity 25.5 Deleting records

You can delete specified records from a databse which match given criteria. Use the STAFF database.

As you have already defined the input and criteria ranges (DEPARTMENT = PERSONNEL), delete all the people in PERSONNEL.

1   SELECT **/ D**(ata) **Q**(uery) **D**(elete) **D**(elete).

2   SELECT **Q**(uit) and look at your database. All PERSONNEL records are deleted and the other records have been moved together.

3   PRESS ALT-F4 if you wish to *Undo* this change.

Key words	Data Query	Find
	Criteria	~
	Criteria range	*
	Input range	?
	Output range	Extract

Database statistical functions

Objective   To examine some of 1-2-3's database statistical functions.

Instructions   There are seven statistical functions in 1-2-3 that can be used with a database.

@DAVG	averages values
@DCOUNT	counts the records
@DMAX	finds the largest value
@DSUM	sums values
@DMIN	finds the smallest value
@DSTD	calculates standard deviation
@DVAR	calculates variance

The general format for these functions is as follows:

@function(input range, offset number, criteria range)

The *input range* is the section of the database used in the calculation.
The *offset number* identifies the field for calculation.
The *criteria range* is where the selection criteria is found.

Activity 26.1

Use the more popular functions with the STAFF database. Work out, for the ACCOUNTS department,

- the average salary
- total salary bill
- the best paid accountant
- the number of employees.

1   SELECT **/FR STAFF** and retrieve the STAFF database.

Name the input and criteria ranges as follows:

2   MOVE to **A3**.

3   SELECT **/ R**(ange) **N**(ame) **C**(reate).

4   TYPE **INPUT** ENTER to accept the name.

5   HIGHLIGHT **A3..G23** ENTER to accept.

6   MOVE to **A25**.

7   SELECT **/RNC**.

8   TYPE **CRITERIA** ENTER.

9   HIGHLIGHT **A25..G26**.

10 CHECK the contents of the criteria range. It will probably contain tests from your previous tasks. To delete them PRESS **/ R**(ange) **E**(rase) **A26..G27**.

11 MOVE to **F26**.

12 TYPE **ACCOUNTS**.

You can now use these two named ranges in your formulae.

13 In A40 TYPE **Average salary in ACCOUNTS department**.

14 In A41 TYPE **Total salary bill in ACCOUNTS**.

15 In A42 TYPE **Best paid accountant**.

16 In A43 TYPE **Number of employees in ACCOUNTS**.

Now enter the formulae:

17 In F40 TYPE **@DAVG(INPUT,4,CRITERIA)**.

18 In F41 TYPE **@DSUM(INPUT,4,CRITERIA)**.

19 In F42 TYPE **@DMAX(INPUT,4,CRITERIA)**.

20 In F43 TYPE **@DCOUNT(INPUT,4,CRITERIA)**.

You will need to format the figures:

21 MOVE to **F40**.

22 SELECT **/RFC2**.

23 HIGHLIGHT **F40..F42**.

The overflow in F41 can be overcome by widening the column (**/WGCS12**) or formatting this cell to currency but with no pence i.e. **/RFC0**.

The following spreadsheet should be shown on your screen:

```
Criteria range:
     A         B          C         D       E         F              G
25 EMPNO FIRSTNAME  SURNAME    SEX     SALARY    DEPARTMENT     DOB
26                                               ACCOUNTS


Results
     A         B          C         D       E         F         Formulas used
40 Average salary in ACCOUNTS department    £15,607.14  @DAVG(INPUT,4,CRITERIA)
41 Total salary bill in ACCOUNTS            £109,250.00 @DSUM(INPUT,4,CRITERIA)
42 Best paid accountant                     £27,5000.00 @DMAX(INPUT,4,CRITERIA)
43 Number of employees in ACCOUNTS                    7 @DCOUNT(INPUT,4,CRITERIA)
44
45
```

Key words	@DAVG	@DMIN
	@DCOUNT	@DSTD
	@DMAX	@DVAR
	@DSUM	

Section H: Data analysis

Task 27   **Creating a frequency table**

Objectives   To create a frequency table.
To revise the creation of a graph.

Instructions   A frequency table places data into a range of categories and counts how many values are in each. It is useful for statistical analysis when there is a need to classify by sex, age, income etc. You can graph the results if you wish. For the purposes of this Task use employee salaries from the STAFF database in Task 24.

Activity 27.1

1   SELECT **/** **F**(ile) **R**(etrieve) **STAFF** if you need to.

You will first set up the salary range intervals - the *bin range*. Each bin represents the upper limit of an interval. For employee salaries the bin category 10000 will include all salaries up to and including £10000.

Look at the range of employee salaries. Choose an interval of £5000, start at £10000 and step upwards to £35000 using **/** **D**(ata) **F**(ill).

2   MOVE to cell **I4** - an empty part of the worksheet.

3   SELECT **/** **D**(ata) **F**(ill).

4   ENTER fill range **I4..I9**.
    Start: **10000** ENTER
    Step: **5000**   ENTER
    Stop: **35000** ENTER

1-2-3 fills the bin range with the specified numeric intervals.

5   SELECT **/** **D**(ata) **D**(istribution).

6   ENTER value range: **E4..E23** - the employee salaries.

Note: the data in this value range can be in any order.

7   ENTER bin range: **I4..I9**.

1-2-3 enters frequency values in column J one column to the right of the bin. So, for example, there are seven employees with salaries greater than £15000 but less than or equal to £20000. The last number shows any values greater than £35000; in this data set there are no salaries above so the value returned is 0.

If you change the values in the salary range, use **/ Data Distribution** again to recalculate the frequency table.

Activity 27.2 Further practise - Graph revision

Create a bar chart of the frequency distribution table. Refer to Task 16 if you need more help.

1 SELECT **/ G**(raph) and from the Graph Settings box: SELECT **Type - Bar**.

2 SELECT Range **A** and the range **J4..J9**.

3 PRESS F2.

4 SELECT **3-D bars**.

5 SELECT **Horizontal grid lines**.

6 SELECT **V**(iew).

Add titles and label the X and Y axes as follows:

7 PRESS ESC.

8 SELECT **Options Titles First**.

9 TYPE in the first line of your graph title - **Frequency Distribution Table**.

10 SELECT **Titles Second**.

11 TYPE in the second line of your graph title - **Employee salaries**.

12 SELECT **Titles X-Axis** and TYPE **Salaries £'000s**.

13 SELECT **Titles Y-Axis** and TYPE **Frequency**.

14 PRESS F10 to view the graph.

Now to improve it.

15 PRESS ESC.

Label each of the 6 bar points on the X-axis with the salary intervals:

16 SELECT the bin range.

17 PRESS ESC. From the Graph Settings box SELECT **RangesX** and ENTER **I4..I9**.

18 SELECT **OK**.

19 PRESS F10 to view.

20 PRESS ESC.

21 SELECT **S**(ave) and name it **Freqdist**.

22 SELECT **Q**(uit).

A **.PIC** file is created which you can print later if you wish.

23 SELECT **F**(ile) **S**(ave) to save these updates to the **STAFF** file.

Frequency Distribution Table

Employee Salaries

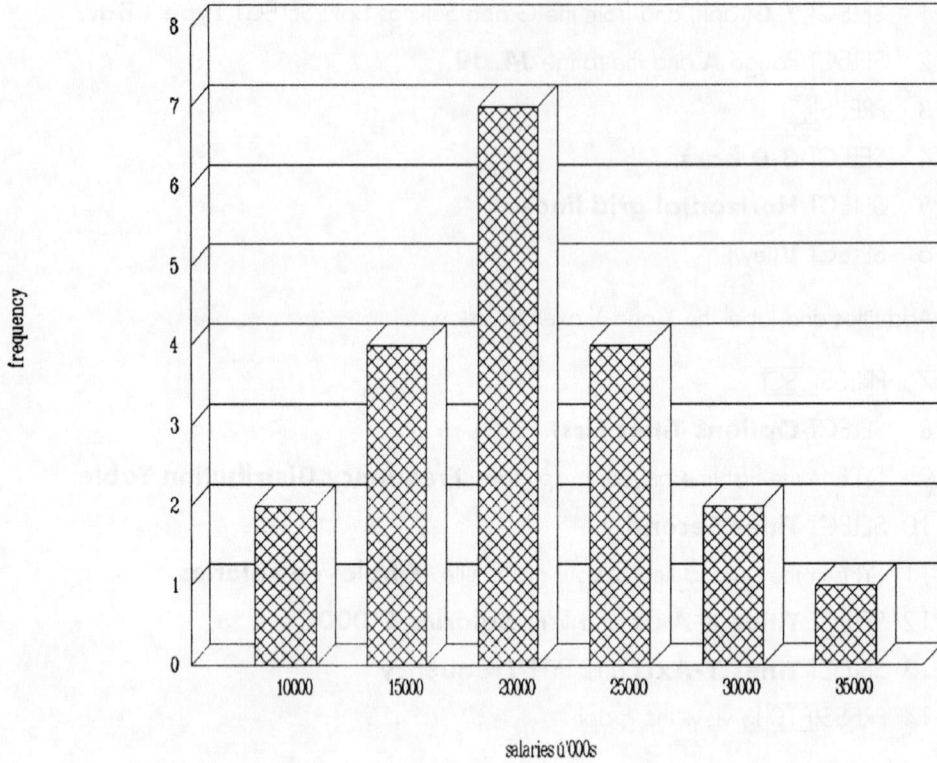

Key words	**Frequency table**
	Bin range
	Data distribution
	3-D bar
	Grid lines

Task 28   **Financial functions**

Objective   To use some of the main financial functions in a worked example.

Instructions   1-2-3 has a number of built-in @functions which can help with financial decision making.

Activity 28.1 Calculating the return on an investment or cost of a loan

Assume that you need to borrow £100,000 to help your business. You can pay back the loan yearly by three payments of £25,000 and finally two of £30,000, as shown below.

@IRR(guess, range) - calculates the internal rate of return expected from cash generated by an investment.

> **guess** is the best guess of rate of return between 0 (0%) and 1 (100%).
> **range** is a series of cash flows; the first value is a negative number.

@NPV - calculates the net present value of future cash flows i.e. what a future sum is worth at today's prices.

> **discount rate** is a fixed periodic interest rate expressed as a decimal or percentage value.

> **range** is a series of future cash flow values.

1   TYPE in the spreadsheet below:

```
        A               B         C          D          E          F
 1                   Estimated cash repayments
 2              Year0    Year1     Year2      Year3      Year4      Year5
 3               -100      25        25         25         30         30
 4
 5 Rate of return (estimate)
 6              12.00%
 7
 8
 9 Net Present Value
10              -3.87
11 @NPV(A6,B3..F3)+A3
12
13 Internal rate of return (IRR)
14              10.5%
15 @IRR(A6,A3..F3)
16
```

Ensure that you:

2   TYPE **-100** in cell **A3** as the initial loan. *Note*: this is a negative value.

3   TYPE **.12** in cell **A6**. This represents your best guess (12%). Format this to percent with **/RFP2**.

4   TYPE **@NPV(A6,B3..F3)+A3** in cell **A10**.

Note: that the initial loan (in A3) is separate as it is not a *future* cash flow affected by the interest. It is added to the result of the @NPV calculation.

5   TYPE **@IRR(A6,A3..F3)** in cell **A14**.

1-2-3 will show an internal rate of return (IRR) of 10.5%. If the IRR is less than 0 or greater than 1 then try another guess value. To determine this, find the net present value (NPV) of the cash flows. If NPV is negative the guess is too high. Similarly, lower your guess if the NPV is positive.

Activity 28.2

Assume you have arranged a £25,000 loan with your bank at 12.5% interest over 5 years. After 2 years of the loan period the bank offer to renegotiate the loan at 10% but the payback period is reduced to 2 more years. Which is the best option for you?

See spreadsheet below.

@PMT(principal,interest,term) will calculate the regular repayments assuming they are equal.
@PV(payments,interest,term) will calculate the present value of investments.

The results are displayed in column D and the underlying formulae are shown as text alongside so that you can TYPE them into your worksheet.

A	A	B	C	D	E	F
1	Loan			25000		£25000 borrowed
2	Interest rate			12.5%		at 12.5%
3	Term (months)			60		five year loan
4	Monthly payment			£562.45		@PMT(D1,D2/12,D3)
5						
6	Principal left after 2 years		£16,812.78			@PV(D4,D2/12,D3-24)
7						
8	After 2 years the bank offers to renegotiate the remainder of the loan:					
9						
10	Interest rate			10.0%		
11	Term (months)			48		over 2 years at 10%
12	Monthly payment			£426.42		@PMT(D6,D10/12,D11)
13						
14	Total payments renegotiated		£33,966.71			(D11*D12)+(D4*24)
15	Total payments original		£33,746.91			+D4*D3
16						
17	Difference			(£219.80)		+D15-D14
18						
19	So the bank's offer is not worthwhile as you stand to lose					
20				(£219.80)		

PMTPRINT.WK1

You can see from the results that you are best to stay with your present loan agreement.

Key words @IRR
@NPV
@PMT
@PV

Task 29　Data analysis with matrices

Objective　To use matrices to analyse data.

Instructions　Matrices can be used to solve problems with many variables. A 1-2-3 **matrix** is a *range* that contains a number in each cell. The number could be a constant in a formula or the coefficient for a variable.

A matrix is defined by its dimensions; hence a 3 by 2 matrix contains three rows and two columns of numbers.

Matrix analysis finds the relationship between two or more sets of variables in one or more formulas. The relationships can help to determine which combination of values will produce the desired result for the formula(e). Activity 29.1 is an example.

Activity 29.1

A brewer considers that there are three main factors that determine beer sales: advertising expenditure, salesforce incentives which encourage the sales team to sell more to outlets such as supermarket and off-licence chains, and promotional offers, including price discounts and customer deals. The following formula represents this relationship:

x% (advertising expenditure) **+ y%** (sales team incentives)**+ z%** (promotion offers) **= Total sales**

Use matrix analysis to determine the percentage contribution each factor makes to overall sales.

1　First SET UP the spreadsheet as shown below:

	A	B	C	D	E
1		Impact on Beer sales			
2					
3		Advertising	Sales team	Promotion	Total
4	Year	expenditure	incentives	offers	sales (£000s)
5	-------	---------	---------	---------	---------
6	1991	12000	3456	8900	112000
7	1992	14000	2341	6700	115000
8	1993	10900	9265	7500	116000
9					

2　SELECT **/ D**(ata) **M**(atrix) **I**(nvert).

3　ENTER range to invert: **B6..D8** 3-by-3 matrix of expenditure for each variable by year. *Note*: The matrix range must have the same number of columns and rows to invert it.

4　ENTER the output range: **A10** is the upper left cell of the range. The inverted matrix results will appear in range **A10..C12**.

These are now multiplied with the sales figures to find the percentage contributions.

5   SELECT **/ D**(ata) **M**(atrix) **M**(ultiply).

6   ENTER first range to multiply: **A10..C12** the inverted matrix.

7   ENTER second range to multiply: **E6..E8** the sales totals.

8   ENTER output range **B15..B17**. The results will appear here.

9   SELECT **/ R**(ange) **F**(ormat) **P**(ercent) **0** to format this range.

10 TYPE in reference labels as follows:

In A15 **Advertising**
In A16 **Sales team**
In A17 **Promotion**

	A	B	C	D	E
1		Impact on Beer sales			
2					
3		Advertising	Sales team	Promotion	Total
4	Year	expenditure	incentives	offers	sales (£000s)
5	---				
6	1991	12000	3456	8900	112000
7	1992	14000	2341	6700	115000
8	1993	10900	9265	7500	116000
9					
10	−0.00015	0.000200	0.000008 <--		inverted
11	−0.00011	−0.00002	0.000156		matrix
12	0.000368	−0.00026	−0.00007		
13					
14					
15	Advertising	63%			
16	Sales team	26%		<--	results
17	Promotion	31%			
18					

You can see that advertising seems to be the main factor affecting beer sales in this case.

Activity 29.2 Solving simultaneous equations with /Data Matrix

You can use **/ D**(ata) **M**(atrix) **I**(nvert) and **M**(ultiply) to solve simultaneous equations. Equations should have the x and y coefficients on one side and the constants on the other.

For example:

$$3x + 5y = 25$$
$$2x + 3y = 21$$

1   CREATE two matrices

    In cells **H7..I8** ENTER the x and y coefficients:

    3 5
    2 3

    In cells **K7..K8** ENTER the constants **25** and **21** respectively.

2   SELECT **/ D**(ata) **M**(atrix) **I**(nvert).

3   ENTER the range to invert: **H7..I8** - the x and y figures.

4   ENTER output range **H10**.

5   SELECT **/ D**(ata) **M**(atrix) **M**(ultiply).

6   ENTER the first range to multiply: **H10..I11** - the inverted matrix.

7   ENTER second range to multiply: **K7..K8** - the constants.

8   ENTER output range: **I14..I15**.

The result will appear in these cells i.e. **x = 30, y = -13**.

9   TYPE in the reference labels: In cell H14 TYPE **x =** ; In cell H15 TYPE **y =** .

```
          G                H                I        J         K
1                    Simulaneous equations
2
3   equations:  3x+5y=25
4               2x+3y=21
5                                                        second range for
6                    x and y coefficients               /Data Matrix Multiply
7   matrices           3                5                    25              I
8                      2                3                    21           <--
9
10                   -3                5      <--         first range for
11                    2               -3                 /Data Matrix Multiply
12
13            solution
14            x =                     30      <--         results of
15            y =                    -13                  /Data Matrix Multiply
16
```

Key word   **Matrix**

Task 30   **Data tables**

Objective   To solve *what-if* problems using 1-2-3's data table facility.

Instructions   *What-if* queries require the analysis of one or more variables to get an answer. Example what if questions might be - *What-if* sales go up by 10% *or What-if* wages rise by 5%?

These problems are easy to solve. You simply adjust the appropriate figure and 1-2-3 will recalculate the results. However, you may want to see the effect on sales of *several* possible changes e.g. 2.5%, 5%, 7.5%. This is where the data table feature will be useful to create and display a list of possible outcomes automatically.

Activity 30.1 Using one-way data tables

A one-way data table is used when you need to assess the effect of different values of one variable. In this Activity the variable is the interest rate on a loan. You will learn how a data table can automatically calculate interest repayments on a £65,000 loan. Two formulae will be used; one for annual and one for monthly repayments.

Examine the worksheet below:

```
A:A1: [W14] 'interest rate                                            READY
Enter name of file to retrieve: C:\123R3\TEMP\DATATAB.WK1
```

A	A	B	C	D	E	F	G
1	interest rate	10.00%			Loan repayments		
2	loan	65000			at various interest rates		
3							
4		6500	541.67		column B - annual payments		
5	10.00%	6500	541.67		column C - monthly		
6	10.50%	6825	568.75				
7	11.00%	7150	595.83				
8	11.50%	7475	622.92				
9	12.00%	7800	650.00				
10	12.50%	8125	677.08				
11							
12							
13							

1   In A1 TYPE **interest rate**.

2   In A2 TYPE **loan**.

3   In B1 TYPE **0.1**. This is the *input cell*.

4   Format this cell to percent by SELECTING **/RFP2**.

5   In B2 TYPE **65000**.

6   MOVE to **A5**.

7 ENTER the various interest rates that you wish to see the results for. TYPE in these input values **10.00%**, **10.50%** etc in cells **A5..A10**. SELECT **/ D**(ata) **F**(ill) to create them if you prefer. Remember to format the range to percent, two decimal places.

8 In B4 TYPE **+B1*B2** - simply a percentage of the loan. Leave column C for now.

9 SELECT **/Data Table 1**.

10 ENTER table range: **A4..B10**. *Note*: the top left cell must be blank.

11 ENTER input cell 1: **B1**.

The interest payments for the six rates will appear in column B. Now add another formula.

12 In C4 TYPE **(B1*B2)/12** to give monthly interest repayments.

13 REPEAT step 9 but WIDEN table range to **A4..C10**.

14 ACCEPT B1 as the input cell. *Note*: the monthly repayments in column C.

15 ENTER the labels in column E to explain the purpose of the table.

Activity 30.2 Using two-way data tables

Examine the following worksheet:

	A	B	C	D	E	F	G
15	interest rate	10.00%			Annual loan repayments		
16	loan	65000			at various interest rates		
17					and loan amounts		
18	6500	65000	75000	100000	column B - £65,000		
19	10.00%	6500	7500	10000	column C - £75,000		
20	10.50%	6825	7875	10500	column D - £100,000		
21	11.00%	7150	8250	11000			
22	11.50%	7457	8625	11500			
23	12.00%	7800	9000	12000			
24	12.50%	8125	9375	12500			
25							

A two-way data table is used when you need to assess the effect of different values of two variables in one formula. In this activity the variables are interest rate (from the last activity) and loan amount.

1 From Activity 29.1 COPY **A1..B10** to **A15**.

2 MOVE formula in **B18** to **A18** - the upper left corner of a two-way table must contain the formula you wish to calculate, in this case +B15*B16 i.e. annual loan repayments.

3   In B18 TYPE **65000**.

4   In C18 TYPE **75000**.

5   In D18 TYPE **100000**.

6   SELECT **/ D**(ata) **T**(able) **2**.

7   ENTER table range: **A18..D24**.

8   ENTER input cell 1: **B15**, the interest rate.

9   ENTER input cell 2: **B16**, the loan amount.

1-2-3 will calculate all eighteen results (6 interest rates x 3 loan amounts) for your evaluation.

10 ENTER the labels in column E to explain the purpose of the table.

11 SELECT **/ F**(ile) **S**(ave) and name your file.

Activity 30.3 A worked example: Break even analysis

Monks PLC plans to sell a new product at £10. The materials and other direct costs to make this product cost £4. The fixed costs, rent and rates, insurance etc will be £75000, however many they make and sell, up to 20000 units.

How many do they need to sell to breakeven i.e. to cover all costs? How many do they need to sell to make a profit of £30000?

See the worksheet below:

	A	B	C	D	E	F	G
1	output (units)	2500			Breakeven analysis		
2	price	10			Variables:		
3	variable cost	4			output		
4	fixed costs	75000					
5							
6		Sales	Variable	Fixed	Total	Profits	
7			costs	costs	costs		
8		25000	10000	75000	85000	-60000	
9	2500	25000	10000	75000	85000	-60000	sales
10	5000	50000	20000	75000	95000	-45000	
11	7500	75000	30000	75000	105000	-30000	
12	10000	100000	40000	75000	115000	-15000	
13	12500	125000	50000	75000	125000	0	Break-
14	15000	150000	60000	75000	135000	15000	even
15	17500	175000	70000	75000	145000	30000	
16	20000	200000	80000	75000	155000	45000	
17							

1   TYPE in the labels in cells **A1..A4** and **B6..F7**.

2   In B1 TYPE **2500**. This is the input cell.

3   In B2, B3, B4 TYPE **10, 4, 75000** respectively.

4   In cells A9..A16 set up the input values from **2500** to **20000** units in steps of 2500 by SELECTING **/ D**(ata) **F**(ill) to do this.

5   In B8 TYPE **+B1*B2**. This formula calculates sales (price x output).

6   In C8 TYPE **+B1*B3**. This calculates variable costs at each output level.

7   In D8 TYPE **+B4**. This simply enters 75000, the fixed costs, from cell B4.

8   In E8 TYPE **(B1*B3)+B4**. This calculates the total costs at each output level.

9   SELECT **/ D**(ata) **T**(able) **1**.

10   ENTER table range: **A8..E16**.

11   ENTER input cell 1: **B1**.

1-2-3 will display the results in columns B..E.

Now add the profits formula:

12   In F8 TYPE **+B8-E8** (sales - total costs).

13   REPEAT step 9 above but WIDEN the table to **A8..F16**.

Note: the breakeven level of output (where total costs are covered) is 12500 units. You can see that the company will have to sell 17500 units to make a profit of £30,000.

Activity 30.4 Create line graph

Now create the graph below. Refer to Tasks 16 and 17 if you need to.

1   SELECT **/ G**(raph) **T**(ype) **L**(ine).

2   SELECT **Options Titles** and enter:
    First title :   **Break even chart**.
    Second title: **Monks PLC**.
    X-axis title: **output(units)**.
    Y-axis title: **£'s**.

3   SELECT **Q**(uit).

4   SELECT **A**.

5   HIGHLIGHT **B9..B16** - the sales figures.

6   SELECT **B** and highlight **D9..D16** - the fixed costs.

7   SELECT **C** and highlight **E9..E16** - the total cost.

8   SELECT **X** and highlight **A9..A16**. This will place the output levels along the x-axis.

9   SELECT **O**(ptions) **G**(rid) **V**(ertical) to draw grid lines up the graph. These are used to highlight the output levels.

10 In G9 TYPE **sales** and in G13 TYPE **Breakeven point**.

11 SELECT **/ G**(raph) **O**(ptions) **D**(ata-Labels) **A** and highlight **G9..G13**.

    Note: that the Breakeven label is the fifth item in the range. This is reflected by its position in the graph.

12 SELECT **A**(bove) to place the label above the sales line.

13 REPEAT steps 10 and 11 for range B data-label (fixed costs, cell A4) and range C (Total costs). EXPERIMENT with the placements of each label to gain the best effect.

14 SELECT **Q**(uit).

15 SELECT **L**(egend) **A** and at the prompt TYPE **sales**.

16 Repeat for B and TYPE **fixed costs** and for C TYPE **total costs**.

    PRESS F10 (graph function key) to view the graph at any time.
    PRESS ESC to return to menu.

17 SELECT **G**(raph) **S**(ave) and name it **BREAKP** to save it as a .PIC file for printing.

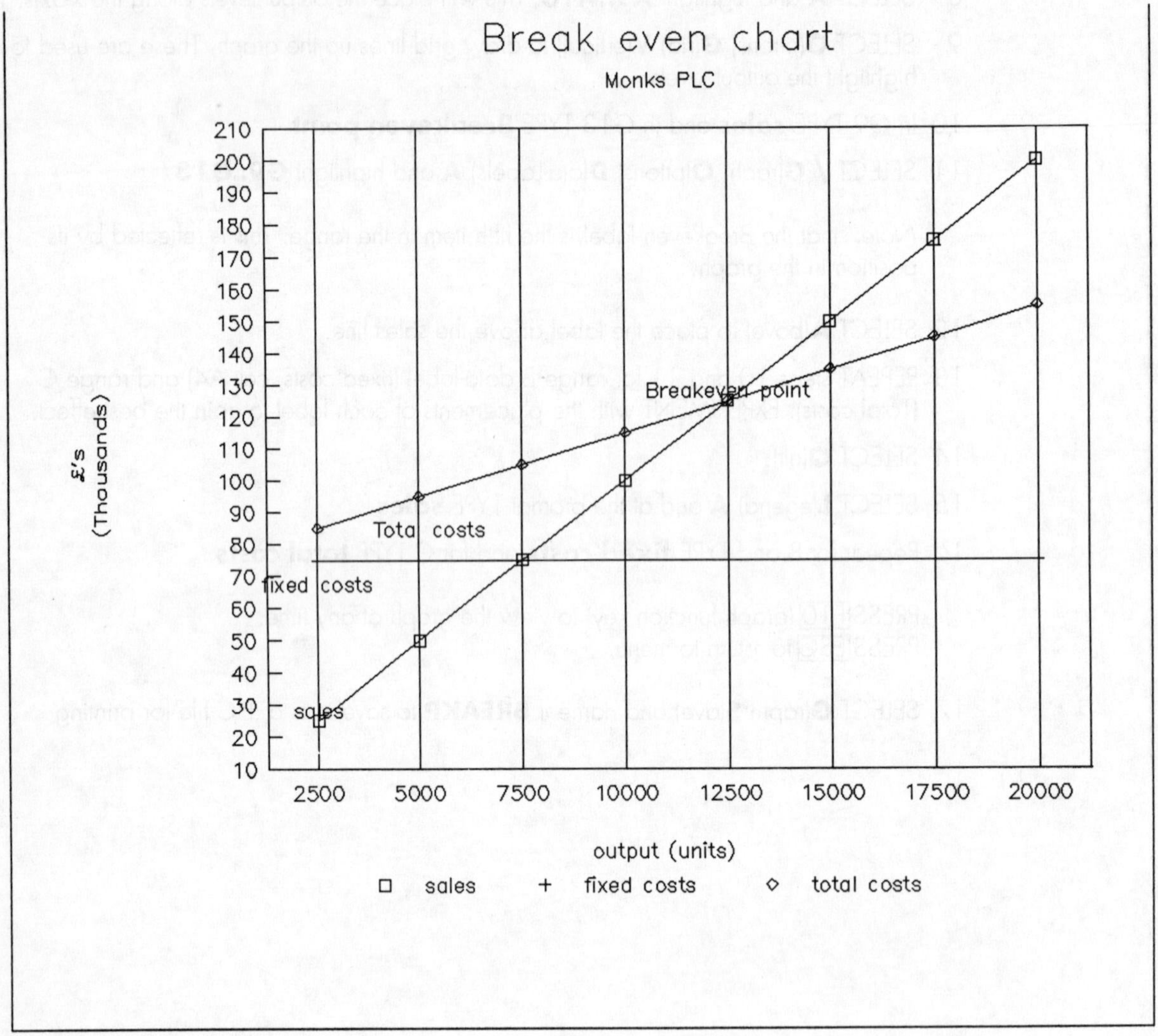
Break even chart
Monks PLC
210
200
190
180
170
160
150
140
130
120
110
100
90
80
70
60
50
40
30
20
10
£'s
(Thousands)
Breakeven point
Total costs
fixed costs
sales
2500
5000
7500
10000
12500
15000
17500
20000
output (units)
sales
fixed costs
total costs

Key words ***What-if***
Data table
One-way table
Two-way table
Break even analysis

Section I: Add-in programs

Task 31 | **The Viewer add-in program**

Objectives   To attach the Viewer add-in program
To browse and retrieve files using it.

Instructions   1-2-3 comes with several add-in programs, one of which is VIEWER.ADN. This program allows you to view the contents of each file on disk together with DOS directory information. Viewer displays files and file contents in two windows. This is useful for file housekeeping and for finding out the contents of old disk files etc.

Activity 31.1 Attaching an add-in

Before you can use Viewer you must first attach it:

1   SELECT **/ A**(dd-In) **A**(ttach).

2   SELECT **VIEWER.ADN** from the list of names.

3   SELECT **N**(o-Key). *Alternatively* you can SELECT a number that represents the key to assign the add-in to. For example, if you assign it to the number 7 you need to PRESS Alt-F7 to activate it.

Activity 31.2 Using Viewer

1   SELECT **A**(dd-In) **I**(nvoke) **V**(iewer).

Three options will appear:

Retrieve   shows the contents of worksheets before you retrieve them
Link   views contents of cells before linking them in the current worksheet. This helps cross referencing and would have made Task 20 easier
Browse   views contents of text files

2   SELECT **B**(rowse).

3   SELECT RIGHT ARROW for tree view.

The **list window** on the left of the screen displays the list of file names in your current directory. These can be sorted in name or date order.

4   PRESS F5 for DATE SORT.

Brackets appear around F5 at the bottom of the screen denoting that the files are in date order, with the most recent first.

5   PRESS [F6] for NAME SORT to sort file names alphabetically. *Alternatively* CLICK the relevant boxes at the bottom of your screen with your mouse. SCROLL through the list with the pointer movement keys.

Note: the contents of the highlighted file appear in the **View window** on the right. Some *Wysiwyg* files (*see* Task 31) may display only characters and symbols.

6   PRESS [ESC] to return to Viewer main menu.

7   SELECT **R**(etrieve).

8   PRESS [RIGHT ARROW].

9   HIGHLIGHT CARS.WK1 and PRESS [ENTER] to retrieve the file.

10 SELECT **/ A**(dd-In) **C**(lear) to remove all add-ins from memory.

Key words **Viewer**
              Add-in
              Retrieve
              Link
              Browse

Working with other programs and files

Objectives To show how to combine and extract files.
To exchange data from 1-2-3 to other programs and vice versa.

Instructions You can extract all or part of a file and copy it to another file.

Activity 32.1 Extracting a file

1   SELECT **/ F**(ile) **R**(etrieve) **CARS**.

You will extract column E for the Turbo model:

2   MOVE to cell **E4**.

3   SELECT **/ F**(ile) **X**(tract) to extract a portion of a file to a new file.

4   SELECT **F**(ormulas).

5   ENTER name of file: **CARSNEW**.

6   ENTER extract range: **E4..E13**.

7   SELECT **/ F**(ile) **R**(etrieve) **CARSNEW** to see the results.

Note: that column A has the Turbo model figures, including adjusted underlying formulae.

Activity 32.2 Combining files

Now make some changes to the CARSNEW file:

1   In A1 TYPE **Sports**.

2   In A3 TYPE **20599**.

3   SELECT **F**(ile) **S**(ave) **CARSNEW R**(eplace).

4   SELECT **/ F**(ile) **R**(etrieve) **CARS**.

5   MOVE to **G4**.

6   SELECT **/ F**(ile) **C**(ombine) to combine all or part of another worksheet file into the current worksheet.

7   SELECT **C**(opy) **E**(ntire-File).

8   PRESS F3 for file list.

9   HIGHLIGHT **CARSNEW**.

The sports car details will be placed in column G starting at cell G4, where you positioned the cell pointer.

Working with other programs and files

1-2-3 allows you to transfer data from worksheet files (in .WK1 format) into other file formats and vice versa. So, for example, you may want to use your 1-2-3 spreadsheet with a word processing file in WORDPERFECT *or* with a database file in dBASEIV *or* with another spreadsheet in SUPERCALC.

Using data from a text file

You can import two types of text file:

- a delimited text file which contains characters like commas that separate data; *or*
- a nondelimited file which does not separate data. *See* the 1-2-3 user guide for further information.

Activity 32.3 To combine imported data with the current file

To combine imported data with the current file first MOVE the cell pointer to a clear area of the worksheet then follow the steps below:

1   MOVE the cell pointer to an empty part of the worksheet.

2   SELECT **/ F**(ile) **I**(mport) to copy data from a text file into the worksheet.

The text file should be in ASCII (American Standard Code for Information Interchange) format. Most personal computer software programs can use data in ASCII format.

3   SELECT **N**(umbers) for text and numbers from a delimited file.

4   SELECT **T**(ext) for text and numbers from a nondelimited file.

5   After the data is in 1-2-3 SELECT **/ D**(ata) **P**(arse) to convert the data into separate columns.

6   PRESS F2 Input, Output to specify these tanges.

7   PRESS F4 to point to ranges in worksheet.

8   SELECT **F**(ormat) **L**(ine) **E**(dit) to arrange column headings.

9   SELECT **G**(o) to parse data.

Parsing imported data

You cannot use the numbers in calculations unless you use **/ D**(ata) **P**(arse) and specify the input column range and output range.

Parsing data converts any long labels into separate columns of data. Refer to the 1-2-3 User Guide for more information on parsing.

Translate

You can create a text file in ASCII format using **/** **P**(rint) **F**(ile). This file can be used in another program e.g. a word processing one or printed with a DOS command.

You can convert 1-2-3 worksheet data to another file format using the *Translate* utility from the Access menu. This means that you can use 1-2-3 data with other spreadsheet and database management programs. Equally *Translate* converts data from other programs into 1-2-3 file format.

Translating worksheets

The source file is the file you want to translate.
The target file is the new file you create.

Activity 32.4 Saving data in a text file

1 SELECT **/** **F**(ile) **P**(rint) **filename**.

2 SPECIFY print range.

3 SELECT **A**(lign) **G**(o).

4 SELECT **Q**(uit) to finish the print job.

Key words **ASCII**
Parse
Translate
Import

Task 33   The *Wysiwyg* publishing add-in and formatting

Objectives   To attach a *Wysiwyg* add-in.
To format a worksheet.

Instructions   *Wysiwyg* (what you see is what you get) is 1-2-3's spreadsheet publishing add-in available for versions 2.3 and 2.4. It can in a number of ways, enhance the appearance of your work, for example, it lets you:

- control screen colours and worksheet fonts
- format data in bold or italics
- set off data with lines or shading
- include graphs in a worksheet

The following Tasks will show you some of its features.

Note: You can always use a mouse to move the cell pointer, display 1-2-3 and *Wysiwyg* menus and select ranges. 1-2-3 displays small pictures (icons) in the icon panel to the right of the worksheet area. Use these pointer-movement icons to move the cell pointer.

Activity 33.1 Starting Wysiwyg

When you attach an add-in it stays in memory until you select **/ A**(dd-in) **D**(etach).

1   SELECT **/ A**(dd-in) **A**(ttach).

2   SELECT **WYSIWYG.ADN**.

3   SELECT **N**(o-Key).

4   SELECT **Q**(UIT) to return to 1-2-3 *ready* mode.

Activity 33.2 Starting Wysiwyg automatically

To start *Wysiwyg* every time you run a 1-2-3 session:

1   SELECT **/ W**(orksheet) **G**(lobal) **D**(efault) **O**(ther) **A**(dd-in).

2   SELECT **S**(et).

3   SELECT **1** as an auto-attach add-in setting (one of the other numbers will do just as well if you prefer).

4   SELECT **WYSIWYG.ADN**.

5   SELECT **N**(o-Key).

6   SELECT **N**(o) if you do not want the Wysiwyg menu to appear automatically; SELECT **Y**(es) otherwise.

7   SELECT **Q**(uit) to return to the previous menu.

8   SELECT **U**(pdate) to save the setting.

9   SELECT **Q**(uit) to return to 1-2-3 *ready* mode.

10 To invoke the Wysiwyg command menu PRESS **:** (colon) or MOVE the mouse into the control panel, then CLICK the right button.

Activity 33.3 Formatting worksheets with Wysiwyg

For the purpose of this Activity use the CARS file.

1   SELECT **/ F**(ile) **R**(etrieve) **CARS** ENTER.

To format worksheets using Wysiwyg, commands may be selected from the Wysiwyg menus using *either* the pointer-movement keys *or* the mouse.

Using the keyboard:
PRESS **:** (colon) **F**(ormat).

Using the mouse:
MOVE the pointer to the control panel.
CLICK **right button on mouse** to toggle between Wysiwyg and conventional 1-2-3 command menu.
CLICK **F**(ormat).

Activity 33.4 Changing a font

Four typestyles are available in 1-2-3: Swiss, Dutch, Courier and Xsymbol. All text is in 12 point Swiss unless you change it.

Now change the titles font for Arthur Daley Motors in the CARS spreadsheet. (Mouse commands are given for this task.)

1   If you have not already done so, MOVE to the control panel and CLICK right to call up the Wysiwyg menu.

2   CLICK **Format**.

3   CLICK **Font**.

4   CLICK **3** for Swiss 24 point.

5   CLICK OK.

1-2-3 prompts for the range:

6   MOVE to **C1** where the title Arthur Daley is.

7   DRAG **C1..C2** and CLICK to highlight the two title lines.

1-2-3 changes font and display.
Note: {Swiss 24} is displayed at the top of the control panel in the two cells.

EXPERIMENT with the other fonts to see what they look like.

Activity 33.5 Bold and italics

1   CLICK **Format Bold Set**.

2   HIGHLIGHT range to embolden: **C1..C2**.

3   CLICK.

4   CLICK **Format Italics Set**.

5   Highlight range: **C2** (just the second title).

6   CLICK.

The titles are now in bold with the second line in bold italics.
Note: **Clear** with the **Set** option cancels these changes.

Activity 33.6   Add a line

1   PRESS F4 *or* DRAG mouse to select B4..F4.

2   SELECT **F**(ormat) **L**(ines) **O**(utline).

1-2-3 puts an outline box around the headings.

3   SELECT **F**(ormat) **L**(ines) **D**(ouble) **B**(ottom).

4   HIGHLIGHT **B16** the Grand Total figure.

5   CLICK.

1-2-3 draws a double horizontal line at the bottom of cell B16.

6   EXPERIMENT with *Format Lines* and see how easy it is to add single and double lines vertically and horizontally.

Activity 33.7 Add a drop shadow

1   SELECT **F**(ormat) **L**(ines) **S**(hadow) **S**(et).

1-2-3 adds a 3-D effect to enhance the appearance:

2   MOVE the title lines from **C1..C2** to **B1..B2** so that they are more central.

3   CLICK **right**.

4   SELECT **M**(ove).
    Move what? C1..C2
    To where? B1

5   SELECT **F**(ile) **S**(ave) and name your file **CARSWYS**

6   Now PRINT your spreadsheet out. It should look like the following:

Arthur Daley Motors
Car Sales for August 19-9

	Basic	Special	GTX	Turbo	Deluxe
1 filename CARS					
6 Basic Price	5995.00	6995.00	10995.00	15495.00	15495.00
7 VAT	1049.13	1224.13	1749.13	1924.13	2711.63
8 Price inc tax	7044.13	8219.13	11744.13	12919.13	18206.63
9 Number plates	25.00	25.00	25.00	25.00	25.00
10 Price on road	7069.13	8244.13	11769.13	12944.13	18231.63
12 Monthly sales	7	10	6	8	2
13 Total sales	49483.88	82441.25	70614.75	103553.00	36463.25
14	1.00	2.00	3.00	4.00	105.00
16 Grand Total	342556.13				
18 Average price	10380.49				
19 Number of models	5				
20 Best seller (value)	103553.00				
21 Worst seller (value)	36463.25				

Key words *Wysiwyg*
Mouse
Font
Bold
Italics
Drop shadow

Task 34   Wysiwyg graphics

Objective   To show how you can use Wysiwyg to add a graph to a worksheet and then to edit and enhance it.

Instructions   For the purpose of this Task, you will use the CARSWYS worksheet file. CALL UP the CARSWYS spreadsheet with **/ F**(ile) **R**(etrieve) if you need to.

Activity 34.1 Adding a graph

You now need to specify the range that will contain your graph. This will determine the location and size of the graph.

1   MOVE to **C16** - an empty area in your worksheet.

2   PRESS ⦂ to call up the Wysiwyg menu.

3   SELECT **G**(raph) **A**(dd) **C**(urrent).

4   HIGHLIGHT range **C16..F21**.

1-2-3 sizes the graph to fit in the range and adds it to the worksheet. This looks a bit small so:

5   SELECT **Z**(oom).

6   PRESS ENTER *or* CLICK on any cell in the selected graph range and note the full screen display.

7   PRESS ESC to return to Wysiwyg menu.

Now increase the graph size in the worksheet.

8   SELECT **S**(ettings) **R**(ange).

9   PRESS ENTER *or* CLICK on any cell in the graph range.

10   HIGHLIGHT **C16..F27** to define the new graph display range.

11   SELECT **Q**(uit) to return to *ready* mode.

Activity 34.2 Enhancing the graph

⦂ Graph Edit commands move you to a graph editing window where you can make enhancements to your graph.

Amend a title
1   PRESS ⦂.

2   SELECT **G**(raph) **E**(dit).

1-2-3 prompts: **Select the graphic to edit:**

3   SPECIFY any cell in the range that contains the graph (DOUBLE CLICK in the graph range if using a mouse).

The **: Graph Edit menu** appears in the control panel and the bar graphic appears in the editing window.

4   SELECT **A**(dd) **T**(ext).

5   TYPE **Forecast Results** ENTER.

Wysiwyg prompts: **Place text:** and shows a cursor **+** in the graphic.

6   POSITION text using the mouse or the pointer-movement keys. Watch the X and Y co-ordinates change. One place to put the extra text would be on line 3 below 'model sales by value'.

7   CLICK or PRESS ENTER to place text.

A small, rectangular box, called a **bounding box**, appears around the text. The text is now part of the graphic.

8   CHANGE the font of the title. SELECT **E**(dit) **F**(ont) **7** for *Dutch* 12 point.

This changes the appearance of your new text. Experiment with font types to find something that suits you.

9   SELECT **Q**(uit) to return to *ready* mode.

10   SELECT **F**(ile) **S**(ave) and name your file **CARSWYS**.

11   SELECT **R**(eplace) to write over the old CARSWYS which did not have any graphics.

Key words **Bounding box**
              Edit font
              ***Wysiwyg* graph**
              Zoom

Task 35   **Wysiwyg text ranges**

Objective   To use text commands to enter text straight into a worksheet.

Instructions   You can use text commands to enter text straight into a worksheet. It can then be editied, aligned and formatted.

You will:

- align a label within a range (instead of within a cell)
- enter text directly into the worksheet
- reformat a range of existing labels

Activity 35.1 Centring a worksheet title over data

1   SELECT **/** **F**(ile) **R**(etrieve) **CARSWYSG** if you need to.

2   MOVE to cell **B1**.

3   PRESS▣.

4   SELECT **T**(ext) **A**(lign) **C**(enter).

Wysiwyg prompts: **Select range to align:**

5   HIGHLIGHT **B1..F1**, the range that you wish to centre within.

The title is centred.
Note: ^ (for centre alignment) appears in the control panel.

Activity 35.2 Entering text directly

1   MOVE to cell **A23**.

2   PRESS▣.

3   SELECT **T**(ext) **E**(dit).

4   Wysiwyg prompts: **Select text range:** HIGHLIGHT **A23..A27** ENTER.

A cursor appears at the left edge of the first cell in the range (A23) and the graphic blanks out (do not worry).

5   TYPE **Here is a copy of the spreadsheet and graph that I promised you for tomorrow's meeting**.

6   PRESS ESC.

The text appears as labels in the specified range with {Text} in the control panel for each cell in the range. The graphic reappears.

Now try changing some of the text.

7 PRESS ▣.

8 SELECT **T**(ext) **E**(dit).

9 The range **A23..A27** is highlighted. PRESS ENTER to accept.

10 CHANGE the word '**tomorrow's**' to '**today's**'.

11 PRESS ESC.

12 SELECT **T**(ext) **R**(eformat) to rearrange the column labels so that it fits within the new text range.

13 SELECT **A23..B27** ENTER to increase the range size.

Note how the text adjusts:

14 SELECT **F**(ile) **S**(ave) and name your file **CARSWYST**.

		Basic	Special	GTX	Turbo	Deluxe
1	filename CARS	**Arthur Daley Motors**				
2		*Car Sales for August 19-9*				
3						
4		Basic	Special	GTX	Turbo	Deluxe
5						
6	Basic Price	5995.00	6995.00	10995.00	15495.00	15495.00
7	VAT	1049.13	1224.13	1749.13	1924.13	2711.63
8	Price inc tax	7044.13	8219.13	11744.13	12919.13	18206.63
9	Number plates	25.00	25.00	25.00	25.00	25.00
10	Price on road	7069.13	8244.13	11769.13	12944.13	18231.63
11						
12	Monthly sales	7	10	6	8	2
13	Total sales	49483.88	82441.25	70614.75	103553.00	36463.25
14		1.00	2.00	3.00	4.00	105.00
15						
16	Grand Total	342556.13				
17						
18	Average price	10380.49				
19	Number of models	5				
20	Best seller (value)	103553.00				
21	Worst seller (value)	36463.25				
22						
23	Here is a copy of the spreadsheet and					
24	graph that I promised you for today's					
25	meeting					
26						

Arthur Daley Motors
model sales by value
Forecast results

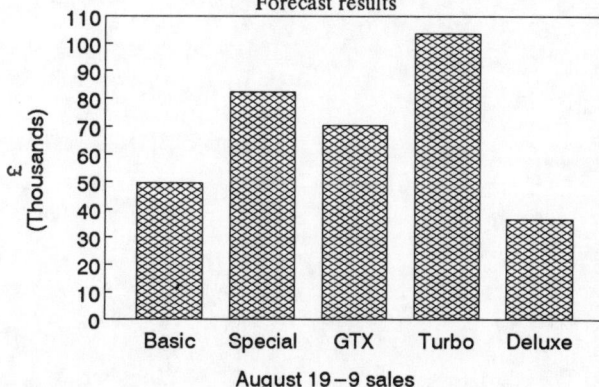

(Thousands)

110
100
90
80
70
60
50
40
30
20
10
0

Basic Special GTX Turbo Deluxe

August 19–9 sales

124

Task 36   **Wysiwyg preview and print**

Objectives   To preview a page before printing.
To specify portrait (across the page) *or* landscape (down the page) printing.

Instructions   Use the spreadsheet, graph and text in the CARSWYS file.
SELECT **/ F**(ile) **R**(etrieve) **CARSWYST** if necessary, to display the file on screen.

Activity 36.1 Previewing and printing a page

1   PRESS ▒ for the Wysiwyg menu.

2   SELECT **P**(rint) **R**(ange) **S**(et) to specify the print range.

3   HIGHLIGHT **A1..F27** to cover all of the figures, graphic and text.

4   SELECT **P**(review) to see what will be printed. The dotted lines are the page margins.

5   PRESS ESC to return to the Print menu.

6   SELECT **Q**(uit)

Note: the dotted lines now outline the print range in the worksheet.

7   PRESS ▒.

8   SELECT **P**(rint) **G**(o) to print.

9   SELECT **Q**(uit) to return to *ready* mode.

Activity 36.2 Getting your printed spreadsheet to fit the paper

Sometimes your spreadsheet can be too wide to print. There are several ways of coping with this.

- Narrow the columns
- Split the spreadsheet and repeat the borders
- Adjust the left and right margins
- Use the compression feature
- Print landscape

It might be feasible to narrow columns either individually or globally so that the data fits across the page. However, do not ruin presentation by cramping data unnecessarily.

1   SELECT **/ W**(orksheet) **G**(lobal) **C**(olumn-Width) *or* **/ W**(orksheet) **C**(olumn) **S**(et-Width) to change the column width.

2   SELECT **: P**(rint) **L**(ayout) **B**(orders) **T**(op). SELECT F4 to move to the spreadsheet and SELECT the cell range containing text to be printed as a top border on every page.

This command sequence allows you to specify borders to print at the top of each page in the print job. Similarly, **: Print Layout Borders Left** specifies the borders to print at the left margin of each printed page.

Repeating labels on each printed page helps to explain figures.

This sets the right margin to 240 characters across.

3   SELECT **L**(ayout) **C**(ompression) **A**(utomatic).

This command compresses a print range so that more data fits on a printed page *or* it expands a print range so that printed data is larger.

Printing across or down the page

Wysiwyg offers portrait (across the paper) or landscape (down the length of the paper). *Note*: you must have a laser printer to use this option if you are using version 2.3. A dot matrix or laser printer can be used with version 2.4..

Portrait is the default, but landscape can be useful for a larger spreadsheet that does not fit neatly across the page.

4   SELECT **C**(onfig) **O**(rientation) **L**(andscape).

The Print settings dialog box is updated and **X** marks landscape orientation within it.

5   PRESS ESC to leave Configuration options and CLICK OK *or* PRESS ENTER.

6   SELECT **P**(review) to see what will be printed.

7   PRESS ESC.

8   SELECT **G**(o) to print.

Key words	Preview	Border
	Portrait	**Margins**
	Landscape	**Compression**
	Layout	

Section J: Add-in programs for 1-2-3 v 2.4 ■■■

Task 37   **The SmartIcons add-in**

Objectives   To use icons.
To add, delete and move icons.

Instructions   This Task assumes that you have the SmartIcons add-in attached. If it is not attached, see Activity 31.1 to find out how to attach it.
The SmartIcons add-in program displays icons (*either* graphic images *or*, if Wysiwyg is not attached, text representing these images). There are 77 icons from which to select to perform 1-2-3 *or* Wysiwyg tasks. To use an icon, you select it using *either* the mouse *or* the keyboard. This Task assumes you are using a mouse. If, however, you are using the keyboard press Alt-F7 (*or* the key you assigned to a SmartIcon to attach it). Then move the highlight to the required icon using the cursor movement keys (ARROWS, END, HOME) and PRESS ENTER to select.

If you want to work on a range be sure to highlight the range before you select the icon.

Icons are organised in **palettes**. A palette is a column of icons which appears on the right hand side of the worksheet. Each palette is identified by a number at the bottom of the column. Click this number with the mouse to move around the palettes.

Getting help
To display a brief description of what each icon does, move the mouse pointer to the icon and hold down the right button. An explanation will appear in the control panel. Move around the icons practising this so that you become familiar with them.

Icon reference table
The most useful icons are shown in the following reference table. The first column shows the icons as they appear in graphics mode when Wysiwyg is attached. Icons in column 2 are as they appear in text mode or when Wysiwyg is not attached. Some icons work only in Wysiwyg indicated by w.

The icons shown are the ones in the guide. There are many others. To get an explanation of an icon's function *see Getting help* above.

Column 1 icons   **Column 2 icons**
Graphics mode   **Text mode**

		Saves the current worksheet to a disk file
		Retrieves a worksheet file from disk

		1+2=	Sums values in a range
W	U	U _	Adds (or removes) a single Underline to data in a range
W	B	B	Displays data in a range in Bold or clears bold
W	A→A	2→2	Displays available Fonts for the highlighted range
			Adds an icon to a custom palette
			Removes an icon from a custom palette
			Moves an icon on the custom palette
		DATE	Enters current date in current cell

Activity 37.1 Using icons with the mouse

The aim of this Activity is to use SmartIcons and the mouse to help create a small file with headings and three numbers which will be summed and the total figure emboldened and underlined. The file will then be saved to disk and then retrieved.

1   TYPE **ILENE DOVER** in A1.

2   TYPE **week 1**, **week 2**, **week 3**, and **Total** into A3, B3, C3 and D3 respectively.

3   TYPE **45**, **89** and **99** into cells A4, B4 and C4 and PRESS ENTER.

4   CLICK in cell D4.

5   CLICK the Sum icon $\begin{smallmatrix}1\\+2\\3\end{smallmatrix}$ on palette 1.

The result should be displayed in cell D4.

6   CLICK Bold icon **B**

7   CLICK the underline icon U

The total is now bold and underlined.

You file should look like this:

```
                  A        B        C        D
1 ILENE DOVER - weekly sales forecast
2
3         week 1   week 2   week 3   Total
4            45       89       99      233
```

8   MOVE the mouse cursor to the File Save icon on the top of palette 1.

9   CLICK **right** for the brief description "saves the current worksheet file to disk".

10 CLICK the File Save icon.

11 At the prompt TYPE in filename **Smartco** and PRESS ENTER.

12 SELECT **/ W**(orksheet) **E**(rase) **Y**(es) to clear the screen.

13 MOVE to the File Retrieve icon and CLICK to retrieve the file.

14 CLICK **SMARTICO.WK1** - the file is retrieved from disk.

Activity 37.2 Adding an icon

You can add or delete icons from the palette to suit your needs. For example, you may wish to display those icons you use most frequently on palette 1.
This procedure will add an icon to your custom palette.

1   MOVE to bottom of palette column and CLICK until you reach palette 6 where the Add-in Icon is. It should look like

2   CLICK Add Icon.

3   MOVE to the Current Date icon on palette 3.

1-2-3 inserts a copy of the icon at the bottom of palette 1. If the palette was full before you added the new icon, 1-2-3 removes the bottom icon.

Activity 37.3 Deleting an icon

1   CLICK on the Del (Delete) icon .

2   CLICK the Fonts icon .

3   CLICK palette number and MOVE to the custom palette.

Note that 1-2-3 has removed the icon from the custom palette.

Activity 37.4 Moving an icon

You can move icons around on your custom palette and group them as you wish. You will now move the Bold icon below the Underline icon.

1 CLICK Move icon ▦↱ from palette 6.

2 CLICK Bold icon **B** from palette 1.

3 CLICK Underline icon U

Experiment freely with the icons. With practise they can provide quick and easy access to many aspects of 1-2-3.

Task 38   The Backsolver add-in

Objective   To use the Backsolver add-in.

Instructions   Backsolver answers what-if questions by changing the value of one or more variables so that the result of a formula matches a particular target value that you want. Use this facility for any 'goal-seeking' exercise where you are asking the question:

'What do I have to do to achieve..?'

This thinking will apply to business applications such as cost control and personnel applications. For example, what sales do I need to achieve a particular profit?

Caution: Backsolver replaces original values. If the UNDO feature is off, make sure that you copy the original figures otherwise they will be lost. If UNDO is on you can use it to restore the original values, assuming that you have not made any other alterations.

Activity 38.1   Using Backsolver to cut costs

1   SET UP the spreadsheet shown below with the heading in A1, expense headings in column A from A3 to A7 and figures in column B and SAVE to disk.

	A	B	C	D	E
1	DOOM and GLOOM - annual budget forecast (£'000s)				
2					
3	Wages	147			
4	Office	25			
5	Marketing	12			
6	Distribution	6			
7	Production	10			
8					
9	Total costs	200			
10					
11	Filename: Backsolv.wk1				
12					

2   In B9 INSERT **@SUM(B3..B7)**.

The total cost figure **200** appears i.e. £200,000.

The boss has decided that the company can only afford to spend £180,000.

3   SELECT **A**(dd-in) **A**(ttach).

4   SELECT **BSOLVER.ADN** and PRESS ENTER.

5   SELECT **8** (Alt-F8 can be used in future to invoke Backsolver).

6   SELECT **I**(nvoke) **BSOLVER** and PRESS ENTER.

7   SELECT **F**(ormula-Cell) and HIGHLIGHT *or* TYPE B9.

8   SELECT **V**(alue).

9   TYPE **180** for the desired result value.

10 SELECT **A**(djustable).

11 HIGHLIGHT *or* TYPE **B3..B7** - the range of cell values Backsolver can change.

12 SELECT **S**(olve).

Note how the costs have been adjusted downwards to meet the target.

13 SELECT **/ W**(orksheet) **G**(lobal) **F**(ormat) **F**(ixed) and TYPE **1** to format all of the figures to 1 decimal place.

The results look like this:

```
             A       B       C       D       E
 1 DOOM and GLOOM - annual budget forecast (£'000s)
 2
 3 Wages          132.3
 4 Office          22.5
 5 Marketing       10.8
 6 Distribution     5.4
 7 Production       9.0
 8
 9 Total costs    180.0
10
11 Filename: Backso2
12
```

14 SELECT **/ F**(ile) **S**(ave) if you wish.

Key words **Formula-cell**
Value
Adjustable

Task 39   **The SmartPics add-in**

Objectives   To use graphics from SmartPics.
             To edit SmartPics graphics.

Instructions   SmartPics is an add-in program which contains many ready-made pictures (graphics).
These can be placed in a 1-2-3 worksheet to add visual interest, emphasise a message
and give a professional look to your work. If Wysiwyg files were saved on hard disk
during installation then SmartPics will have been automatically transferred to the 1-2-3
directory. Otherwise, attach it using the procedure in Task 31.

SmartPics are stored in files with the suffix .CGM. For example, the file AIRPLANE.CGM
contains a picture of an aeroplane.

Practise using SmartPics. Add, move and remove graphics. You can also resize and
enhance graphics using :Graph Edit.

Activity 39.1 Using graphics from SmartPics

1   SELECT **/ F**(ile) **R**(etrieve) **BACKSO2**.

2   SELECT **/ F**(ile) **D**(irectory), TYPE **C:** and PRESS ENTER.

This is so that the .CGM files can be retrieved from the hard disk.

3   In D4 TYPE **This is still too high** (This is a message for the office manager.)

4   SELECT **: G**(raph) **A**(dd) **M**(etafile).

5   SELECT **ARROW.CGM**.

6   MOVE to C4 and PRESS ENTER. This is where you wish the graphic to appear.

7   SELECT **A**(dd) **M**(etafile).

8   PRESS F3 for a full screen display of files.

9   SELECT **MONEYBAG.CGM**.

10 HIGHLIGHT **C9..C10** for the graphic range.

11 SELECT **A**(dd) **M**(etafile) F3 **POTGOLD.CGM**.

12 HIGHLIGHT the range **D9..D11**.

13 SELECT **Z**(oom) **C9** or **C10**. This shows a full screen display of the Moneybags
      graphic.

14 PRESS ESC to return to worksheet.

Continue to the next Activity.

Activity 39.2 Moving a SmartPics graphic

Now move the computer graphic from Activity 39.1 upwards.

1 SELECT **/ M**(ove).
2 At the prompt Move what? **C9..D11**.
3 MOVE to C6.

You have now moved the money bag and potgold graphics upwards.

Activity 39.3 Resizing a graphic

You can make a graphic larger or smaller.

1 SELECT **: G**(raph) **S**(ettings) **R**(ange).
2 CLICK or PRESS ENTER on potgold graphic.
3 Extend range from D6..E11.
4 PRESS ENTER.

Activty 39.4 Editing a SmartPics graphic

1 SELECT **: G**(raph) **A**(dd) **M**(etafile) **COMPUTER.CGM**.
2 ENTER graphic display range **F2..H13**.
3 SELECT **Edit**.
4 CLICK on the computer graphic or PRESS ENTER.
5 SELECT **A**(dd) **T**(ext).
6 TYPE **a very clever PC**. PRESS ENTER.
7 POSITION text on the computer screen using cursor control keys or mouse and PRESS ENTER to confirm.
8 SELECT **Q**(uit) to return to the worksheet.

The worksheet should now include your message on the screen of the computer graphic.

9 SELECT **/ P**(rint) **R**(ange) **S**(et) **A1..H13**. SELECT **G**(o) to print the worksheet and graphics using Wysiwyg.
10 SELECT **/ F**(ile) **S**(ave) **SMARTPIC** to save the file if you wish.

Your file should look like this:

DOOM and GLOOM – annual budget forecast (£'000s)

Wages	132.3
Office	22.5
Marketing	10.8
Distribution	5.4
Production	9.0
Total costs	180.0

This is still too high

a very clever PC

Filename: Smartpic

Key words **Graphic**
Metafile

Section K: Macros

Task 40   Creating macros

Objectives
To outline macros and their uses.
To create a macro to complete cells with standard entries.

Instructions
You can automate any Task in 1-2-3 by creating a macro. A macro is a series of instructions - keystrokes and commands - that can be saved and used over and over again.

Macros are useful for:

- repeated tasks requiring accuracy
- frequently used labels, numbers and formulae
- selecting command sequences
- prompting a user for typing input
- testing cell entries and performing actions based on those entries
- building command menus

There are four basic steps to creating a macro:

1	PLANNING	objectives - plan what you want to do
2	ENTERING	type macro instructions into the worksheet
3	EXECUTING	carry out instructions
4	DEBUGGING	correct errors

When **planning** the macro you need to decide where to put it and what instructions to write in it. There are two ways of creating a macro. You can type it in *or* you can get 1-2-3 to record your keystrokes as you perform the task in *learn* mode. You will type in a macro first and then try the *learn* method in the next task.

To **enter** a macro, type your commands in a column of cells leaving a blank cell to end. Macro instructions can use one or more rows.

- Breaking up instructions on separate rows makes them easier to read.
- Blank rows are *not* allowed (Blank means end of macro).
- It is conventional to type the macro away from the standard worksheet area.

Writing macro instructions

- TYPE **'** to start a macro (*or* any label prefix - **"^**) e.g . **'^1st Quarter**
- To MOVE the pointer use braces, e.g. {right}
- Tilde (**~**) stands for ENTER
- PRESS ENTER to move instructions from the command line to the worksheet

Refer to the 1-2-3 reference book for further macro instructions.

Activity 40.1 Your first macro example

1 ENTER the following as *text*. You may also TYPE in a brief explanation of what the macro does alongside in a separate column - *see* comments below.

Note: these are *not* part of the macro, simply an onscreen description.

		TYPE	**Comments**
In cell	A2	**'Selling costs~**	enters label.
In cell	A3	**'/WCS14 ~{right}**	sets column A width to 14, RIGHT ARROW.
In cell	A4	**'/RFC2~{END}{DOWN}~**	sets column B format to currency with 2 digits.
In cell	A5	**'100~**	enters number.
In cell	A6	**'{goto}A8~**	puts cell pointer at A8.
In cell	A7		leave as a blank cell.

To name a macro:

2 SELECT **/ R**(ange) **N**(ame) **C**(reate).

3 TYPE **macro1**.

4 ACCEPT the range of the macro (**A2..A7** in this case).

5 MOVE to **A1** and TYPE **macro1** ENTER to show the macro name.

Alternatively, a macro can be named with **** and one letter, e.g. **\M** allows you to invoke the macro with ALT-M. The letters and number keys may be used but 0 is reserved for automatically-invoked macros.

Activity 40.2 Executing the macro

Execute (invoke) your macro as follows:

1 MOVE to cell **A8** - the start cell for our display.

2 PRESS ALT-F3.

3 SELECT the macro to run: **macro1** ENTER.

The following will appear on your screen:

	A	B	C	D
1	macro1			Comments
2	Selling costs~			enters label
3	/wcs 14~{right}			sets column width to 14, RIGHT ARROW
4	/rfc2~{end}{down}~			sets column B format to currency with 2 decimal
5	100~			enters number
6	{goto}a8~			puts cell pointer at A8
7				leaves a blank cell
8	Selling costs	£100.00		

To execute a macro step-by-step:

4 PRESS ALT-F2 for *step*.

5 PRESS ALT-F3 and SELECT the macro to run.

6 PRESS any key after each step.

7 PRESS ALT-F2 again to resume normal operation.

This process is useful for finding bugs.

8 To save your macro SELECT **/FS** ENTER and the macro will be saved with the worksheet.

Key words **Macro**
~ (tilde)
prefix
braces

Task 41   **Interactive macros, macros for selecting comands and the macro learn feature**

Objectives   To create interactive macros for entering keyboard data.
To create macros for 1-2-3 command sequences.
To use 1-2-3's macro *learn* facility.

Instructions   Interactive macros are useful for creating "form-filling" routines. Pausing for, and accepting input requires special macro syntax. {?} causes macro execution to pause for input. Tilde (~) - the automatic return - shows that the $\boxed{\text{RETURN}}$ key is expected after user-input before the macro execution will resume. Again, use ' (or any label prefix) to start a macro instruction.

Activity 41.1

1   CLEAR the screen with **/WE Y**(es).

2   TYPE in the following macro in column A.

```
       A          B          C              D              E          F

 1 APPLCATION FORM {D}            APPLICATION FORM
 2 {D}
 3 Enter name:{R}                 Enter name:            {?}
 4 {R}
 5 {?}{D}                         Enter birthdate    @date({?})
 6 {D}
 7 {L}
 8 {L}
 9 Enter birthdate:{R}
10 {R}
11 @date({?})~
12 /rfd~
13 /wcs10~{d}
14
15 Sample result:
16
17 APPLICATION FORM
18
19 Enter name:      Fred
20
21 Enter birthdate:      12-Dec-55
```

3   SELECT **/RNC** and NAME the macro **APPLIC**.

4   PRESS $\boxed{\text{ENTER}}$ to accept the range **A1..A13**.

Again it may be helpful to have brief explanatory comments on screen alongside the macro and the macro name clearly displayed for reference.

To execute the macro:

5   MOVE to cell **D1**.

6   PRESS ALT-F3 and HIGHLIGHT **APPLIC**. Note that the macro pauses in cell F3.

7   TYPE in (**your name**) then PRESS ENTER.

The cursor moves to F5 and **@date** will appear in the command line.

8   TYPE in **your birthday** in YYMMDD format e.g. **55,10,08** would give 08-Oct-55.

9   SELECT **/FS** to save the macro with the worksheet if you wish.

Activity 41.2 Selecting commands

Macros can be used for the automatic selection of 1-2-3 command sequences.

1   TYPE in the following in column AA:

In cell AA1   **'/WGFC0~** - Worksheet Global Format Currency 0.
In cell AA2   **'/RFC2~{Esc}{End}{Left}.{End}{Right}~** Range Format Currency 2.

2   SELECT **/RNC** and name it **FORMAT**.

3   ENTER a few numbers into your worksheet to test it.

4   GO TO cell A1.

5   SELECT **/ D**(ata) **F**(ill).

6   ENTER fill range **A1..E10 Start: 1 Step 1: End** ENTER.

7   In A1 PRESS ALT-F3 to run FORMAT.

Note: this macro sets the worksheet format to currency, with no decimal places, but allows 2 decimal paces on line 1 i.e. the line in which the macro is invoked.

8   SELECT **/FS** if you wish to save the file.

Activity 41.3

Set up a macro to split the window horizontally and set the global column width to 6.

1   TYPE into cell: AA1   **Window macro**.
                      AB2   **'/WWH~**   - split window horizontally.
                      AB3   **'/WGC6~~**   - set global column width to 6.

2   SELECT **/RNC WINDOW** and accept range **AB2..AB3**.

3   GO TO cell **A10**.

4   PRESS ALT-F3 to execute macro.

5   PRESS F6 to move between windows.

6   SELECT / W(orksheet) W(indows) C(lear) to clear the window setting.

Activity 41.4 Using the macro learn feature

An easy way to create macros is to get 1-2-3 to record your keystrokes as you do them so that they can be used again. This involves 4 steps:

(1) SETTING up a column (the learn range) to record your keystrokes.
(2) PRESSING ALT-F5 to turn on learn.
(3) ENTERING your macro.
(4) PRESSING ALT-F5 again to switch off learn.

You will now create a macro to enter a record company's name and sales headings as shown below.

A:B15:   READY

	A	B	C	D	E	F	G	H
1	Heading	r{BS}				Description:		
2	macro	R.STORNAWAY{D}				enters company name		
3		PRODUCT SALES £000s{D}				and product sales		
4		{D}				headings		
5		LPs{R}						
6		SINGLES{R}						
7		CDs{D}						
8								
9								
10		Result:		R.STORNAWAY				
11				PRODUCT SALES £000s				
12								
13				LPs	SINGLES	CDs		
14								
15								
16								
17								
18								
19								
20								

STORNAWA.WK1

1   In A1 TYPE **Heading**.

2   In A2 TYPE **macro**.

3   SELECT **/ W**(orksheet) **L**(earn) **R**(ange).

4   SELECT **B1..B7** [ENTER].

1-2-3 will display the macro instructions in this range when you finish using learn. Usually you do not know how big your macro will be so use more cells than you think you will need.

5   MOVE to **B10**.

6   PRESS [ALT-F5] to turn on learn.
Note: the learn indicator at the bottom of your screen. From now on all of your keystrokes will be recorded:

7   In B10 TYPE **R. STORNAWAY** and PRESS [DOWN ARROW].

8   In B11 TYPE **PRODUCT SALES £000s** and PRESS [DOWN ARROW] twice.

9   In B13 TYPE **LPs** [RIGHT ARROW].

10 In C13 TYPE **SINGLES** [RIGHT ARROW].

11 In D13 TYPE **CDs** [DOWN ARROW].

12 PRESS [ALT-F5] to finish *learn* and PRESS [ENTER].

13 SELECT **/ R**(ange) **E**(rase) **B10..D13** to erase your input.

Before you can use a macro, name it:

14 SELECT **/RNC** and call it **HEADING**.

15 ENTER range as **B1..B7**.

16 MOVE to **D10**.

17 PRESS [ALT-F3] and accept **HEADING** as the macro to execute.

The company headings will appear as specified in the macro at this location.

18 SELECT **/ W**(orksheet) **L**(earn) **C**(ancel) when you finish recording a macro. Otherwise, 1-2-3 will keep adding keystrokes to the range whenever you turn on the *learn* feature.

Key words   **Learn**
                Macro

Case study: The Hot-Stuff Heating Company

Objective   To bring together and revise many of the topics covered in Tasks 1 - 36.

The problem Jack Sharpe, sole proprietor of the Hot-Stuff Heating Company, with capital of £6500 in his bank and an anticipated legacy which he will invest in the business, plans to produce and sell a superior gas fire for next winter. His plans for the business are as follows:

1   He will produce 60 gas-fires a month but expects sales to start from 30 in July, increasing in steps of 10 until October and then in steps of 20 in November and December when he reaches 100 per month.

2   The fires will sell for £180 each but his customers' accounts will only be settled in the third month after the month of purchase.

3   His overheads will be £1000 a month, paid one month in arrears.

4   In September he will pay for the £20,000 of equipment, machinery and computers, he is to buy to start up the business.

5   In November, his solicitor has advised him, he should receive a legacy of £30,000 from the Brazilian estate of his long lost uncle.

6   His unit production costs, which it is not anticipated will rise in the period under review, will be as follows:

    Materials   £50
    Labour   £40
    Variables   £30

7   He will buy materials as needed, paying for them two months later; labour will have to be paid for in the month of production as will his variable costs.

8   Interest charges on the previous month's overdraft will be debited at a rate of 1.5% (one and a half percent) per month. In order to satisfy his bank manager that his request for a £20, 000 overdraft facility will be sufficient to meet the needs of his enterprise in its start-up phase, he needs to draw up a cash-flow forecast for the first six months of operations: that is from July until December.

Activity 42.1 Use 1-2-3 to create the cash-flow table that Jack's bank manager will want to see before granting him the overdraft facility he has asked for. A suggested format for the cashflow forecast is shown on the next page.

   You should produce not only the print of the table as seen on the screen but also, in case the bank manager questions the derivation of the figures, a print showing the underlying formulae used in its production!

```
          A       B        C        D        E        F        G
 1  THE HOTSTUFF HEATING COMPANY
 2  Cash Flow Analysis for 19-8
 3  ======================================================================
 4                  JUL      AUG      SEP      OPC      NOV      DEC
 5
 6  Cash in Bank
 7  ----------------------------------------------------------------------
 8  CASH INFLOW
 9
10  Sales Volume
11  Unit Price
12
13  Sales Income
14  Legacy
15
16  Sub-total in
17  ----------------------------------------------------------------------
18  CASH OUTFLOW
19
20  Prod'n Volume
21  Unit Costs:
22     materials
23     labour
24     variables
25
26  Total Prod'n Costs
27
28  Fixed O'heads
29  New machinery
30  Overdraft charges
31
32  Sub-total out
33  ----------------------------------------------------------------------
34  C/F to Bank
35  ======================================================================
```

The problems of success

By October Jack Sharpe finds that the business is proceeding very much as he had
planned and that advance orders suggest that sales are likely to be maintained at the
December level during January and February, falling to 50 or 60 in March. This is
extremely encouraging but leaves Jack with the problem of how he is going to be able to
satisfy the demand.

His production capacity of 60 gas-fires a month has been sufficient in the start-up
phase because his stocks have been sufficient to cope with the November/December
demand but over the colder months of winter he anticipates that stocks will need to be
increased.

Overtime working, which will inevitably increase his labour costs, seems to be called for and Jack starts to think about how this can be organised.

Weekday and Saturday morning overtime will cost him time and a half, Saturday afternoon and Sunday morning, double time. With the employment situation as it is and Christmas on the horizon, his workforce will be glad of the overtime but Jack's problem is how much, when and how this will affect his overdraft?

After his experience with the first cash-flow analysis, Jack has discarded the idea of guessing what his needs will be and has decided to extend the analysis until April. He has accordingly asked you to do some *'what if'* analysis for him.

Activity 42.2   Use 1-2-3 and, with your existing model as a starting point, extend the analysis until April and investigate some of the possibilities open to Jack. You may assume that only the labour cost will be affected by the overtime working and should remember that selling machines Jack has not produced is not an acceptable means of improving the cash-flow!

To ensure that you have a record of the consequences of the alternative strategies you have investigated, print copies of the sheets with sub-headings to indicate what strategy you are examining.

Appendix I

Using 1-2-3 functions

This section gives a brief overview of some of the most useful business functions found in LOTUS 1-2-3. Functions make formulae more powerful. There are more than 50 to choose from and you can only really learn about them and their various applications by trying them out.

They can be categorised as follows:

- statistical
- mathematical
- logical
- data management
- error trapping
- data arithmetic
- financial
- database statistical
- string

Function syntax

A function has three parts:

prefix	**@**
name	e.g. **AVG**
argument	e.g. **(C2..C7)**

Different functions have different arguments. A few have no argument at all.

e.g. **@SUM(A1..B10)**   argument is a range

     @TODAY   no argument

     @IF(A1>0,B1,C1) conditional followed by two variables

Statistical functions

There are eleven of these:

@COUNT	counts the number of items
@SUM	adds the values
@AVG	finds the average
@MIN	identifies the minimum value
@MAX	identifies the maximum value
@STD	calculated the standard deviation
@VAR	calculates the variance
@ABS	converts negative numbers to positive
@INT	returns the integer (whole number) part of a number
@ROUND	rounds a value to a specified number of decimal places. e.g. @ROUND(1.337) = 1.34 to two decimal places.
@RAND	generates a random number between 0 and 1.

A list of cells must be specified as the argument. A simple list would just be one cell or range of cells e.g. **@SUM(B2..B7)**. However, you can include more than one cell or range like this: **@SUM(B2..B4,B6..B8,B10..B12,B15,B20)**
Empty cells are ignored. Labels will have a value of 0.

Logical functions

@FALSE	indicates or returns a value of 0
@TRUE	indicates or returns a value of 1
@IF(condition,x,y)	IF condition is true returns x; IF false returns y

@IF   can be used in many ways to produce results based on
                         evaluation of data in other cells.

For example, suppose the number of hours worked was held in cell B2, overtime was
paid at time-and-a-half if hours exceeded 40 and the hourly rate was in C2. The formula
for calculating weekly pay would be:
@IF(B2>=40,(B2-40)*C2*1.5+40*C2,B2*C2).

@ISERR(x) assigns a value of 1 if x is an acceptable value.
@ISNA(x) assigns a value of 1 if x is an unavailable value.

Data man-   These retrieve data from lists and tables.
agement   **@CHOOSE(x,v0,v1,v2,..)**   chooses the xth value in a list.
functions   **@HLOOKUP(x,range,n)**   looks up values in horizontal tables.
    @VLOOKUP(x,range,n)   looks up values in vertical tables.

e.g. **@VLOOKUP(525,A4..E7,3)** uses 525 as the test (lookup) value, A4..E7 as the
table range and 3 as the offset value i.e. the number of columns along.

Error   These allow you to flag omissions or errors.
trapping   **@NA**   means not available
functions   **@ERR**   means error, not acceptable.

Date and   Dates entered as ordinary labels cannot be used directly in formulae or functions as they
time   have *no numeric value*. Hence functions are used that generate serial date and time
functions   numbers.
    @DATE(year,month,day) is used to enter dates; it assigns a numeric value to each
date to allow arithmetic operations.
@DATEVALUE(date string)   the date number of date string.
@NOW   serial number for current date and time.
@TIME(hr,min,sec)   cf **@DATE**.
@TIMEVALUE(time string)   cf **@DATEVALUE**.
Functions that use serial date and time numbers:
@DAY(date number) extract day from year number
@MONTH   extract month from year number
@YEAR   extract year from year number
@HOUR   extract hour
@MINUTE   extract minute from time number
@SECOND   extract second from time number
@TODAY   assigns the date from the DOS date entry

Financial   These calculate such things as loans, annuities, cash flows and depreciation rates over a
functions   period of time. They include:
@CTERM(int,fv,pv)   the number of compounding periods needed for an investment
    of *present value* (pv) to grow to *future value* (fv) earning a fixed
    periodic interest rate inv.
@FV   for *future value* and **@PV** for *present value* of an annuity.
@NPV(int,range)   the *present value* of the series of future cash flows in a *range*,
    discounted at the *periodic interest rate* (int).

@IRR(guess,range)		the *internal rate of return* for the series of cash flows in the *range* based on the approximate percentage *guess* of the IRR.
@PMT(prin,int,term)		the amount of the periodic payment needed to pay off *principal* (prin) at *periodic interest rate* (int) over the number of payment periods in *term*.
@RATE(fv,pv,term)		the periodic interest *rate* necessary for *present value* (pv) to grow to *future value* (fv) over the number of compounding periods in *term*.
@SLN(cost,salvage,life)		the *straight line* depreciation allowance of an asset for one period given the *cost*, the predicted *slavage* value and *life* of the asset.

String functions (see Task 26)	**@CHAR**	shows a character not on the keyboard
	@EXACT	determines if two character strings are the same
	@FIND	finds a smaller string in a larger one
	@ISSTRING	determines if a cell entry is a label
	@LEFT	takes the left characters
	@LENGTH	determines the length of a string
	@LOWER	converts upper case letters to lower case
	@MID	midstring
	@PROPER	converts a string to a proper case
	@REPEAT	shows multiple copies of a string
	@REPLACE	replaces or inserts text
	@RIGHT	takes the right characters
	@STRING	converts a number to a string
	@TRIM	removes blank spaces from a string
	@UPPER	converts lower case to upper case
	@VALUE	converts a string to a number.

Appendix II

Answer to Task 42, Activity 42.1

Entering the model

TYPE in all the labels as suggested. Use the repeat key for the line separaters.
SELECT **/WCS17** to widen column A for the long labels.
SELECT **/RLR B4..G4** to right-justify the monthly headings.

The rest involves formulae work and copying, all of which you have met before.

SELECT **/WGFF2** to format all the cells to two places of decimals. In B6 TYPE **6500**.
TYPE the unit sales figures into cells **B10..G10** (*see* note 1 on page 143).
SELECT **/RFF0 B10..G10** for whole numbers.
In B11 TYPE **180** and COPY into **C11..G11**.
In E13 TYPE **+B10*B11** (i.e. July's income received 3 month's later (*see* note 2 on page 143)).
COPY the formula into **F13..G13**.
In F14 TYPE **30000** (the legacy - *see* note 5 on page 143).
In B16 TYPE **@SUM(B13..B15)** to add Sales and other income.
COPY across into **C16..G16**.
In B20 TYPE **60**.
COPY to **C20..G20**.
SELECT **/RFF0 B20..G20** for whole numbers.
In B22 TYPE **50**.
In B23 TYPE **40**.
In B24 TYPE **30**.
COPY **B22..B24** to **C22..G24**.
In B26 TYPE **@SUM(B23..B24)*B20** (materials excluded - see note 7 on page 143).
COPY into **C26**.
In D26 TYPE **@SUM(D22..D24)*D20**.
COPY into **E26..G26**.
In C28 TYPE **1000**; COPY into **D28..G28**.
In D29 TYPE **20000** (see note 4 on page 143).
In B32 TYPE **@SUM(B26..B31)** to add all the outgoings.
COPY the formula into **C32..G32**.
In B34 TYPE **+B6+B16-B32** (i.e. cash at start plus cash received minus cash paid out).
COPY into **C35..G35**.
In C6 TYPE **+B34**. This simply copies the carried forward cash balance from the end of the previous month to start the new one.
COPY into **D6..G6**.
SELECT **/WCS10** to widen columns D, E and F so that the figures are in view.

Now return to the overdraft in row 30.

In B30 TYPE **@IF(B6<0,@ABS(B6*0.015),0)**.
COPY this into **C30..G30**.

This formula means:
IF the balance at the start of the month (B6 for July) is <0.
    THEN multiply that balance by 1.5% ignoring the minus sign (the
@ABSolute function).
    ELSE 0 - ie no overdraft charge as you are in credit.

Note: that without **@ABS** you would be paying out less. Think about it! Your bank
manager would not be happy! The results and the full contents list are shown below so
that you can check your work.

	A	B	C	D	E	F	G
1	THE HOTSTUFF HEATING COMPANY						
2	Cash Flow Analysis for 19-8						
3	==						
4		JUL	AUG	SEP	OCT	NOV	DEC
5							
6	Cash in Bank	6500.00	2300.00	-2900.00	-31143.50	-34410.65	-5926.81
7	--						
8	CASH INFLOW						
9							
10	Sales Volume	30	40	50	60	80	100
11	Unit Price	180.00	180.00	180.00	180.00	180.00	180.00
12							
13	Sales Income				5400.00	7200.00	9000.00
14	Legacy					30000.00	
15							
16	Sub-total in	0.00	0.00	0.00	5400.00	37200.00	9000.00
17	--						
18	CASH OUTFLOW						
19							
20	Prod'n Volume	60	60	60	60	60	60
21	Unit Costs:						
22	materials	50.00	50.00	50.00	50.00	50.00	50.00
23	labour	40.00	40.00	40.00	40.00	40.00	40.00
24	variables	30.00	30.00	30.00	30.00	30.00	30.00
25							
26	Total Prod'n Costs	4200.00	4200.00	7200.00	7200.00	7200.00	7200.00
27							
28	Fixed O'heads		1000.00	1000.00	1000.00	1000.00	1000.00
29	New machinery			20000.00			
30	Overdraft charges	0.00	0.00	43.50	467.15	516.16	88.90
31							
32	Sub-total out	4200.00	5200.00	28243.50	8667.15	8716.16	8288.90
33	--						
34	C/F to Bank	2300.00	-2900.00	-31143.50	-34410.65	-5926.81	-5215.71
35	==						

Answer to Activity 42.1

A1:[W17] 'THE HOTSTUFF HEATING COMPANY
A2:[W17] 'Cash Flow Analysis for 19-8
A3:[W17] \=
B3:\=
C3:[W10] \=
D3:[W10] \=
E3:[W10] \=
F3:[W10] \=
G3:\=
B4:"JUL
C4:[W10] "AUG
D4:[W10] "SEP
E4:[W10] "OCT
F4:[W10] "NOV
G4:"G4
A6:[W17] 'Cash in Bank
B6:6500
C6:[W10] +B34
D6:[W10] +C34
E6:[W10] +D34
F6:[W10] +E34
G6:+F34
A7:[W17] \-
B7:\-
C7:[W10] \-
D7:[W10] \-
E7:[W10] \-
F7:[W10] \-
G7:\-
A8:[W17] 'CASH INFLOW:
A10:[W17] 'Sales Volume
B10:(FO) 30
C10:(FO) [W10] 40
D10:(FO) [W10] 50
E10:(FO) [W10] 60
F10:(FO) [W10] 8
G10:(FO) 100
A11:[W17] 'Unit Price
B11:180
C11:[W10] 180
D11:[W10] 180
D11:[W10] 180
E11:[W10] 180
F11:[W10] 180
G11:180
A13:[W17] 'Sales Income
E13:[W10] +B10*B11
F13:[W10] +C10*C11
G13:D10*D11
A14:[W17] 'Legacy
F14:[W10] 30000
A16:[W17] 'Sub-total in
B16:@SUM(B13..B15)
C16:[W10] @SUM(C13..C15)
D16:[W10] @SUM(D13..D15)
E16:[W10] @SUM(E13..E15)
F16:[W10] @SUM(F13..F15)
G16:@SUM(G13..G15)
A17:[W17] \-
B17:\-
C17:[W10] \-
D17:[W10] \-
E17:[W10] \-
F17:[W17] \-
G17:\-
A18:[W17] 'CASH OUTFLOW
A20:[W17] 'Prod'n Volume
B20:(FO) 60
C20:(FO) [W10] 60

D20: (FO) [W10] 60
E20: (FO) [W10] 60
F20: (FO) [W10] 60
G20: (FO) 60
A21:[W17] 'Unit Costs
A22:[W17] '   materials
B22:50
C22:[W10] 50
D22:[W10] 50
E22:[W10] 50
F22:[W10] 50
G22:50
A23:[W17] '   labour
B23:40
C23:[W10] 40
D23:[W10] 40
E23:[W10] 40
F23:[W10] 40
G23:40
A24:[W17] '   variables
B24:30
C24:[W10] 30
D24:[W10] 30
E24:[W10] 30
F24:[W10] 30
G24:30
A26:[W17] 'Total Prod'n Costs
B26:@SUM(B23..B24)*B20
C26:[W10] @SUM(C23..C24)*C20
D26:[W10] @SUM(D22..D24)*D20
E26:[W10] @SUM(E22..E24)*E20
F26:[W10] @SUM(F22..F24)*F20
G26:@SUM(G22..G24)*G20
A28:[W17] 'Fixed O'heads
C28:[W10] 1000
D28:[W10] 1000
E28:[W10] 1000
F28:[W10] 1000
G28:1000
A29:[W17] 'New machinery
D29:[W10] 20000
A30:[W17] 'Overdraft charges
B30:@IF(B6<0,@ABS(B6*0.015),0)
C30:[W10] @IF(C6<0,@ABS(C6*0.015),0)
D30:[W10] @IF(D6<0,@ABS(D6*0.015),0)
E30:[W10] @IF(E6<0,@ABS(E6*0.015),0)
F30:[W10] @IF(F6<0,@ABS(F6*0.015),0)
G30:@IF(G6<0,@ABS(G6*0.015),0)
A32:[W17] 'Sub-total out
B32:@SUM(B26..B31)
C32:[W10] @SUM(C26..C31)
D32:[W10] @SUM(D26..D31)
E32:[W10] @SUM(E26..E31)
F32:[W10] @SUM(F26..F31)
G32:@SUM(G26..G31)
A33:[W17] \-
B33:\-
C33:[W10] \-
D33:[W10] \-
E33:[W10] \-
F33:[W10] \-
G33:\-
A34:[W17] 'C/F to Bank
B34:+B6+B16-B32
C34:[W10] +C6+C16-C32
D34:[W10] +D6+D16-D32
E34:[W10] +E6+E16-E32
F34:[W10] +F6+F16-F32
G34:+G6+G16-G32

Answer to Activity 42.2

	A	B	C	D	E	F	G
1		THE HOTSTUFF HEATING COMPANY					
2		Cash Flow Analysis for 19-8					
3	===						
4		NOV	DEC	JAN	FEB	MAR	APR
5							
6	Cash in Bank	-34410.65	-8726.81	-10857.71	-11220.58	-7988.89	1691.28
7	---						
8	CASH INFLOW:						
9							
10	Sales Volume	80	100	100	100	50	60
11	Unit Price	180.00	180.00	180.00	180.00	180.00	180.00
12							
13	Sales Income	7200.00	9000.00	10800.00	14400.00	18000.00	18000.00
14	Legacy	30000.00					
15							
16	Sub-total in	37200.00	9000.00	10800.00	14400.00	18000.00	18000.00
17	---						
18	CASH OUTFLOW:						
19	Opening stock	60	60	40	20	0	10
20	Prod'n Volume	80	80	80	80	60	60
21	Closing stock	60	40	20	0	10	10
22	Unit Costs:						
23	materials	50.00	50.00	50.00	50.00	50.00	50.00
24	labour	40.00	40.00	40.00	40.00	40.00	40.00
25	Overtime (1.5)	60.00	60.00	60.00	60.00	60.00	60.00
26	variables	30.00	30.00	30.00	30.00	30.00	30.00
27							
28	Total Labour cost	3600.00	3600.00	3600.00	3600.00	2400.00	2400.00
29	Total Prod'n Costs	10000.00	10000.00	10000.00	10000.00	7200.00	7200.00
30							
31	Fixed O'heads	1000.00	1000.00	1000.00	1000.00	1000.00	1000.00
32	New machinery						
33	Overdraft charges	516.16	130.90	162.87	168.31	119.83	0.00
34							
35	Sub-total out	11516.16	11130.90	11162.87	11168.31	8319.83	8200.00
36	---						
37	C/F to Bank	-8726.81	-10857.71	-11220.58	-7988.89	1691.28	11491.28
38	===						

Assumptions:

1 Production volume is increased to 80 units from November to February inclusive.
2 The extra output can be paid at time and a half.
3 Sales are 50 in March and 60 in April.

Notes on workings:

1 Extend all labels, formulae and lines by copying.
2 Insert rows to show stock levels and labour costs.
3 Closing stock = Opening stock + production volume - sales.
4 Total labour cost calculations:
    @IF(B20<=60,B24*B20,(B20-60)*B25+60*B24)
      i.e. IF output is less than or equal to 60 then multiply it
      by £40 per unit, ELSE multiply extra output by time and a half
      (£60) plus 60 units at standard rate.